HOPE reclaimed

a plan
and hope
for the future

by
Dr. John A. Marshall

Outskirts Press, Inc.
Denver, Colorado

Hope Reclaimed
A plan and hope for the future

Outskirts Press, Inc.
http://www.outskirtspress.com

Paperback ISBN: 978-1-4327-5566-9
Hardback ISBN: 978-1-4327-6302-2

Library of Congress Control Number: 2010932734

PRINTED IN THE UNITED STATES OF AMERICA

To Gloria
Whose ability to plumb the depths of life
with an unusual faith, intellect, and wit
has brought great joy
in our
fifty years of living together

Table of Contents

ACKNOWLEDGEMENTS vii
ABBREVIATIONS & DEFINITIONS.................................... ix

PART 1: The Need, The Program, A Christian's Opportunity
1

PREFACE: THE JOURNEY OF LIFE.................................... 3
CHAPTER 1: THE STORY OF THE DEVELOPMENT OF
    STEWARDS INC.. 7
CHAPTER 2: THE MINISTRY OPPORTUNITY 15
CHAPTER 3: SOCIAL SECURITY ADMINISTRATION 25
CHAPTER 4: BALANCING AUTONOMY AND
    BENEFICENCE 35
CHAPTER 5: EXPECTATIONS AND RESULTS OF THIS
    FAITH-BASED PROGRAM.................................... 43
CHAPTER 6: LEADERSHIP.................................... 55
CHAPTER 7: THEOLOGICAL AND BIBLICAL BASE FOR
    THIS MINISTRY.................................... 65
CHAPTER 8: A FAITH-BASED AGENCY ACCEPTING
    FEDERAL FUNDS.................................... 77
CHAPTER 9: SUMMARY.................................... 93

Part 2: A Guide for Developing a Representative Payee
Organization
97

GUIDE TO DEVELOPING A FAITH-BASED
    REPRESENTATIVE PAYEE ORGANIZATION................ 103
BIBLIOGRAPHY 129

ACKNOWLEDGEMENTS

Many extraordinary people have been instrumental as encouragers of the development of the faith-based Representative Payee Organization called Stewards Inc. They have also been cheerleaders in my efforts to write this book.

Gloria, my wife, has partnered throughout the adventure. Her creativity and hard work are evident every step of the way, from when we started this ministry out of the back of our car, to the office, staff, and beneficiaries we have today. Her editing this book is more than hovering over grammar, but the sharing of a dream that it will have value in furthering a ministry that has proved redemptive in Bakersfield.

The Bolthouse family, encouraging Stewards Inc for years, shares the dream of ministering to people in other cities by supporting the writing, printing, and dissemination of this book.

Dr. Ray Bakke, Chancellor of Bakke Graduate University of Ministry, has been a friend and supporter since 1980 when we met in Kinshasa, Zaire. His inspiration and belief in urban ministries was seminal in the 1997 development of Stewards Inc.

Dr. Randy White of Bakke Graduate University and Dr. Wesley Brown, missionary, pastor and teacher, have always shared their word of advice and encouragement when needed.

Kelly McKinsey, Stewards Inc's Office Manager and CFO, has been our colleague and steady rock in the development of the office procedures, systems and in the training of the staff. Her great spirit and skills have been foundational to Stewards Inc.

Numerous readers have commented on the manuscripts leading up to this book and their critiques have been very helpful. Now, Hayley Beck, as the final reader, has put her skills to work to make certain the book is in order.

The Stewards Inc's staff, both past and present, has wonderfully served as the translators of my dreams and of God's hope for our clients, both past and present. They are God's chosen people for such a time as this.

Stewards Inc could not have progressed over the years without the encouragement of the local Social Security office and the mentoring of Donna Warren, District Manager. Likewise, this ministry could not have expanded without the support of Wells Fargo Bank and the creativity of Ed Taylor, the South Valley President.

The Board of Directors for Stewards Inc under the leadership of three different Presidents, David Chenot, Beverly Allen, and now Ed Taylor, has been truly foundational in this ministry's birth and development and is now being courageous in guiding the development of Stewards Inc satellites in other cities.

ABBREVIATIONS & DEFINITIONS

Beneficiary – The challenged or differently abled individual receiving Title II, SSA, SSI or VA benefits.

Challenged or Incapable – SSA terminology designating an individual that is unable to manage his or her income funds.

Client Representative – An individual working with beneficiaries in the RPO office.

COLA – Cost of living adjustment.

DAA – Drug and alcohol addiction.

EIN – Employer's Identification number supplied by IRS.

FICA – Federal Insurance Compensation Act.

FBCO – Faith-Based Community Organization.

FBO – Faith-Based Organization.

IRS – Internal Revenue Service (federal).

KCMH – Kern County Mental Health.

LSS – Lutheran Social Services.

Representative Payee – An individual working privately to help manage the SSA income of one or more beneficiaries.

RPO – A Representative Payee Organization, with a letter of approval from the SSA, managing the income of those who are deemed challenged or incapable.

RSDI – Retirement, Survivors, and Disability Insurance. This program is based on the earnings of workers and is commonly called Social Security.

Social Security – A social insurance program that protects workers and their families from a loss of earnings because of retirement, death, or disability.

SSA – The Social Security Administration.

Social Security office – A local office that is assigned to service the citizens of a certain area designated by zip codes.

SSI – Supplemental Security Income. A federal income maintenance program for aged, blind, and disabled persons of all ages who are challenged or incapable.

Title II – Federal old age, survivors and disability insurance program. This represents the Social Security deduction taken out of worker's pay checks and later being dispersed a benefit for retirement.

VA – Veterans Administration.

PART 1
The Need
The Program
A Christian's Opportunity

The Journey of Life

As we are growing up, most of us begin to yearn for adventure. Early childhood tales of *20 Thousand Leagues Under the Sea, Robin Hood,* and *Star Wars* feed our imaginary heroic scenes. We expect that those kinds of events will become the markers of our lives. As we mature and the reality of our life's paths unfold, we discover it is the mundane everyday encounters that create the journey and the most meaningful adventures often involve the simple giving of ourselves to others.

The stirrings of this book began many seasons and episodes of life before the creation of Stewards Inc, as my experiences and call to ministry were molding me. Africa set the geographical stage for my early chapters of feeding the hungry and helping to develop a more abundant life for others. The following snapshot gives a peak into one event.

The crush of humanity on every side made this milestone a sensory experience. In the tropical heat one could smell, feel and hear the excitement of the event. Within my view was a technicolor scene I would later see in black and white photos reproduced in news magazines and cited as a historical event in the turbulent post-independence years in Congo, Africa.

I was working with the United Nations, on loan from my mission, providing food for Baluba tribal people in the Kasai Province of Congo. Albert Kalonji, a government official had just arrived on the grassy airstrip in a C47 aircraft in our small town of Bakwanga.

I joined the swarm of people at the airfield who surged from the surrounding grasslands and forests for the excitement of seeing the plane land. He emerged from the dark interior into the humid glare of mid-afternoon, splendidly attired in a full leopard skin with the forelegs attached to the shoulder seams of his dark blue woolen western suit.

Kalonji had come to declare the Kasai an independent state from Congo, and himself as the Emperor in charge. His booming words in Tshiluba were electrifying as the crowd rushes forward in response. Rough hands on both my shoulders lifted me above the fray and onto the hood of an army jeep full of Baluba soldiers. "Stay here so you are safe," hissed the man in charge. I could barely understand his words, but I shared his concern since I was the only white face in the throng of thousands. As the jeep slowly moved forward, it carved a path in the field of people behind the kipoy carrying the new Emperor and provided a front row seat for me in this amazing historical drama.

The declared empire was short lived and my sojourn as a United Nations rescue worker was equally brief and I was soon back in the city of Leopoldville and into more of life's amazing trails.

The metaphor of "Life as a Journey" makes more sense as the events of one's own life play out and the years are walked through. Many cultures have found their special own ways and words to describe the adventure of life. In South Africa, in the 1800s, when pressed by the arrival of new English settlers who took away some of the freedoms of their life in an ungoverned land, the Dutch farmers started out to reclaim their new self-determination by going on what they termed, "The Great Trek" into the unexplored interior of that part of Africa. History subsequently dubbed them the Boer Trekkers.

The Australians, picking up a habit from the Aborigines who were the first people to live on that piece of land, go on a "walkabout" when needing some time out or adventure. Americans tend to simply "take a hike." No matter what the idiom is used for the trip, the result is the same. Life unfolds, as we move forward, in amazing episodes using the stimulus of people, nature, friendships, work, worship and a Sovereign God behind the scenes to bring meaning. The choices of how one walks and cares for others in our pathways usually determines the quality and joy of the sojourn.

The book that I seek to share on these pages is the record of a more recent milestone experience that has become the warp and woof of my life story these past few years and is separated by a lifetime of episodes from that Congo incident. It is written for those who practice the art of ministry, designed for "Practitioners," if you will; those who dream the impractical and sometimes offbeat ideas for making this a better world one person at a time and then go forward to live out the idea. It outlines an idea for creative ministry to a needy population, complete with a guide in Part 2 for those who might find the challenge compelling enough to try it on. It is not written for theologians, sociologists, or others looking for theoretical answers to possible conundrums, but it is theologically and sociologically sound. Hopefully, this can be a practical tool as well as an inspiration for translating God's promise to freely give a plan and hope for a future into real lives that are often muddy.

CHAPTER 1

The Story of the Development of Stewards Inc

Thus, the purpose of this book is to bring you along on my journey of ministry and to outline both the "how and why" you might choose to organize a ministry for some of the challenged people of your community by creating a Representative Payee Organization through the Social Security Administration. The SSA distributes checks to over 7,500,000 people in the United States who are declared sufficiently disabled to be unable to support themselves. At least twenty percent or 1,500,000 of these recipients are unable to use this income responsibly. They struggle with mental illness, homelessness, addictions, and/or other disabilities that create a need for help.

The SSA program of having a "Representative Payee" help them with budget and financial choices is the springboard that inspired this program. Our experience has shown this tool can be redemptive for folks in need when managed with a caring heart. The goal is to lead clients on the path to a more abundant life as they are guided with the dignity and respect they deserve.

In 1997, 13 years ago, Stewards Inc was started as a RPO with eight beneficiaries, with only my wife and me involved as staff. We were shocked to discover how many people, who needed this helping hand were hidden away in old motels, under bridges, living in abusive situations, or struggling with destructive habits.

Fast forward to 2010 and the statistics look different. After some action packed years and a fast learning track there are now 20 staff members and 1,600 beneficiaries.

The Rescue Mission was a good place for me to volunteer in 1997 when retirement from the pastorate freed up my time. Actually, a lot more time than I was comfortable with having. Being familiar with the Mission, I visited the Director and he asked me to form a crew out of the men staying at the Mission and paint the buildings inside and out. Having always worked with my hands and people, this fit the bill.

As I worked with the crew, I could not help but have memory flashes that took me back to 1942, when I was a boy and my family lived in New Castle, Pennsylvania. My family was invited by my father's boss to a service at the First Baptist Church to hear a visiting evangelist. It was our family's first time in church. The message spoke to the need in my heart and I responded to the invitation to become a person of faith.

Within three days the pastor contacted me and asked that I come to the church office. He said with assurance, "Now that you are a Christian, you need a ministry. I am assigning you to work at the Rescue Mission for two hours after school, five days a week." I was familiar with the Rescue Mission since I helped with the cleaning in a meat market across the street from the Mission on Saturdays. Soon I was too involved for my cleaning job and the Mission became my ministry for the next two years until we moved to California. As I made beds and waited on tables I heard, for the first time, the stories of lives in tumult and met men who had often lost hope for a better life. That experience began to frame the career and ministry paths my life would take.

Back to the present of 1997, a dozen men volunteered to paint. We organized and went to work. I enjoyed the work and the banter that took place as we worked. Abruptly, on the first of the month, however, almost all of those on the crew disappeared only to reappear a few days later. I was curious as to where they went and what they were doing, but everyone kept their silence. It happened again on the first of the next month, so it was time to ask questions and listen a little more carefully. I discovered most of the men were on SSI (receiving disability checks from Social Security). A couple of them were leaving to visit their wives and children and share some of the funds, but the majority of the money was being used for drugs, alcohol and female companionship. As a pastor I had compassion, concern and words of advice, but as a taxpayer I didn't appreciate the way Social Security money was often being used.

Soon the good news of my free labor and skills spread to other non-profits in town. The Director of "Friends Outside" a group providing help to families of prisoners asked if I would repair the electrical components and supervise the painting of their offices. As I climbed around on ladders in that office, I became an automatic part of the conversations and everyday business, whether invited or not. Keeping my mouth shut and ideas to myself, not being my biggest asset, I was soon asking questions and offering advice, even if no one wanted it.

I learned that one of their ministries was to manage the Social Security incomes of the families on disability. Friends Outside had been approved by the SSA to receive the checks and directly pay the rent and utility bills and disperse the remaining funds for food and personal needs to the designated beneficiaries. They were using the Social Security Administration's Representative Payee program.

It made good sense to use the SSA program as a way to guide the use of taxpayer's support for food, shelter and clothing for those who were too challenged to be gainfully employed. Having spent some years living under other government systems, it made me grateful, again, to live in a country that gives aid to the citizens who need it to survive.

All of the beneficiaries' income that was received at Friends Outside was being directly deposited into one global bank account.

From this account, checks were being written to pay rents, bills and fines. Checks for food and other needs were also being written to individuals on demand. Legitimate questions were often asked by the beneficiaries, "How much money do I have left in my account this month?" and "Are you sure that my money isn't being given to someone else?" Volunteers as well as staff were able to write checks when requested, and it was apparent that no one could answer those questions with certainty.

The day came when Social Security audited the books and closed their operation because they were not able to balance each individual check received with checks being written for the benefit of that individual. There was no fraud on the part of Friends Outside, just poor bookkeeping. Those whose checks were involved were abruptly left without a RPO to help them. Unfortunately, kind hearts did not automatically translate into good managers.

Eight of the men, with whom I had built a relationship and trust level, met me as I left the building and asked if I would take on the task of managing their disability checks. I visited the Social Security office and received a booklet on the process of being a RPO. I began a quick study of the responsibilities and risks, and brushed up on my skills of balancing a meager household budget with being able to live healthfully.

My antennae had been out, searching for God's next open door for making a difference in others lives, and this seemed a simple task. Time would reveal that I had a very naïve view of both the tasks and rewards.

Determined to set up a better system than the one I had seen, and to succeed in shining the light on a better life for those for whom I became a Representative Payee, I tackled the problem of partnership with a bank. After a lot of negotiations I found a bank that would open eight individual fiduciary accounts without limits or charges for their services.

Realizing how little I knew of the lifestyle of the men I had brashly assured I could help, my next intensive study was launched.

Several weeks and pairs of shoes later, I had walked the length of Union Avenue where miles of old and crumbling motels lined the street. At one time the entrance corridor to our city, this area had been deteriorating for 50 years since Interstate 99 had bypassed it and cut a new swath into Bakersfield. The drivers of the autos and trucks going both north and south, found new motels along the up-dated route and left the old area to deteriorate and become one of the major sources of low income housing. The oldest profession in the world also found it a profitable area in which to ply its lures.

Eventually, I had talked with the owner or manager of just about every motel. Most were now renting on a weekly or monthly basis to attract low income tenants. They were frustrated over the use of drugs and alcohol in their facilities, but their greatest problem was convincing renters to actually pay their rent. It was a constant battle to collect rents, evict people and find new tenants. More money was going into that struggle than into maintaining and upgrading the buildings, noted the managers, and the proof of that statement was evident everywhere one looked.

Motel rooms of those earlier eras were usually small cubicles, each with an outside door. My next self-assigned task was to talk to the renters. I went door to door, knocking and talking with people. I had to do a lot of reassuring that I was not a probation officer, child or adult protection person or a dealer of some sort. Many of the single renters admitted they moved from motel to motel to avoid paying rent. Families were stuffed into too small a space with be-longings surpassing square footage. I found an unbelievable number of Seniors, many of whom had lost contact with their families, who were not being well cared for. Almost all complained about the roaches, rodents, lack of working air-conditioning and general dete-rioration of the plumbing, roofs and doors.

A lesson I learned very early in this game was to allow benefi-ciaries to choose their own housing. They were rarely neither happy nor apt to stay where I suggested they might live, unless they chose the place and I guaranteed the rent to the landlord. I had some clout to suggest that the proposed apartment or room needed to be cleaned and painted before the person moved in.

My wife and I were the whole organization at this point. She wrote the checks and balanced the accounts while I kept the necessary records and delivered the checks out of the back of my car. It was a great "face to face" and personal way to start and I could assess how each client was really faring each time I saw him.

Soon those eight men discovered that it was a good thing to have someone interested in their lives, caring and praying with them about their problems. I was also trying to shoot straight with them about their need to be responsible with their limited funds and choosing food instead of booze with the remainder after the rent was paid. We tried to connect those who were willing with churches and support groups so their lives could continue to ameliorate. It was good enough, in fact, that they began to round up their friends and bring them to me to help bring about some changes in their lives. As some of our folks began to bloom, the local Social Security office personnel began to make referrals to us.

Before long, the kitchen table, home phone and trunk of my car didn't really cut it to keep up with a system that needed an office and more man hours. We moved into a small office downtown and hired our first helper. A young and capable man with a loving heart, the first thing he asked was, "Where is the computer?" He put us on a fast track to the way things really are organized in this century.

Another staff member joined the team shortly thereafter, bringing new skills and insights. That began the new joy of a parallel track of relationships and partnership with others who shared our hearts for folks who struggle keeping balance in a challenging world. I suppose, if we are honest, we always recognize ourselves as just one small step away from the same syndrome.

By the time we had maxed out four credit cards to cover our office expenses, SSA awarded us a Letter of Approval and required us to charge each client a prescribed fee for our service. Not the fast track to riches, even with more clients, but our little ministry began to balance itself out and with government approval of our 501(c)3 non-profit status, other supporters began to emerge along with a talented and dedicated Board of Directors and the partnership of United Way.

Our lives have been interwoven with hundreds of people over the past few years because of Stewards Inc. The life stories of some of those folks are heroic, some are tragic, but all are part of the fabric of the rich adventure that God has allowed us to enjoy. Together with a wonderful, dedicated staff of workers, we have shared tears and laughter over the life situations we have helped clients live through.

In the ensuing years this organization has grown to presently serving 1,600 beneficiaries, maintaining 1,600 bank accounts, employing 20 staff members, and managing about $2,000,000 monthly of incomes, savings, and reserved funds.

From 2004 to 2009, I had the opportunity of studying at the Bakke Graduate University of Ministry. As we studied in Seattle, Los Angeles, Beijing, New York, and Chicago, it was enlightening and inspiring to study what churches and agencies were doing to help revitalize their communities. At the same time, because there was never mention of a RPO working in these communities, I realized we had developed a unique ministry that brings change to a community.

The dissertation I wrote at the end of this period of study is entitled, "A Bridge to a More Abundant Life for Challenged People, Creating a Faith Based Representative Payee Organization." This book is based on that dissertation.

It must be remembered that the goal is to develop more than an organization. The goal is to ignite hope and inspire futures in those who are challenged and marginalized in our communities.

CHAPTER 2

THE MINISTRY OPPORTUNITY

The Outward Signs Demonstrating a Need for This Ministry

Five years ago. Sylvester was diagnosed as paranoid schizophrenic. Today, he goes to a doctor every two weeks for an injection to help control this condition. His greatest fear is that he will forget the appointment, return to acting out in public, and end up in 3B, the psyche ward at the county hospital.

The fear is justified because of years of struggle and suffering. Sylvester was born 40 years ago in East Los Angeles, CA, where his neighborhood was rough and gang laden. At age nine, his mother and father separated. He says that life changed and things like Thanksgiving and Christmas were gone from his life. His mother raised his sister while he was raised by his father until age 16. At that age, he went to live with his mother in Sacramento, CA, but it was too late. Drugs, alcohol, gangs and violent behavior had become his way of life.

When he was 18 he married, but in a few years his wife, tired of the drug activity, wanted to take their child and leave. Struggling with his undiagnosed mental condition and drugs he ran over his family with a car and spent 6½ years in prison. A parole violation added additional years.

Sylvester says that at this point he blanked out, was homeless, lost direction, couldn't get home and ended up in a park in Bakersfield, CA. Five years ago he was diagnosed as a paranoid schizophrenic and was awarded Social Security disability.

In June 2007, because of his acting out, a Social Security representative stopped his disability check until he signed up at Stewards Inc. When he first came to this ministry, he was not taking his meds and was dirty and homeless. It took time, but patience, encouraging words, a place to live, and money for food brought change to his life.

Today, Sylvester is nicely dressed, exudes a special charisma, has an apartment, and enjoys life. He attends Victory Outreach Church. When we talked about his prayer life he said, "If you are going to have answers to your prayers, you have to work with God. I want to work with God."

Sylvester was one of 53,050,000 individuals who were recipients of a check from at least one of the SSA programs in the month of March 2010. The total of all checks was $56,600,000,000.

The question is, "How many of these recipients of income from Social Security are capable of managing their income?"

Thirty years ago, 5.2 percent of the beneficiaries of all SSA programs were considered too challenged to manage their income, needed help, and were brought into the newly established Representative Payee Program. At first this program required challenged recipients of SSA income to find a family member or friend to help them manage their finances. It soon became clear that family members and friends were not always trustworthy or capable. The next step was approving non-governmental RPOs to manage this income.

Eleven years ago, in 1999, the percentage of those too challenged to manage their income from the SSA had increased to 13.3 percent. Today that percentage has risen to almost 20 percent and is continuing to rise. Basically, SSA estimates somewhere around 40 percent of those receiving income from SSA programs need guidance because of one challenge or another.

The basic premise for the Representative Payee program remains the same. *Beneficiaries who are unable to manage or direct the management of their money need a payee.*[1] If beneficiaries are misusing their retirement or disability income in such a way they are endangering themselves, another, or another's property, they must find a person or agency who will take the responsibility of helping them manage this income. Capable friends and family are encouraged to assume this responsibility. Unfortunately for some challenged individuals, trustworthy or capable family members and friends are not available; therefore, the SSA requires them to select a RPO to help them manage their income. At this point, a faith-based RPO, as a ministry, can meet this need.

Looking back at Sylvester's life, there were four major outward signs showing he needed a RPO to help him manage his income and indirectly help him manage his life. They were homelessness, substance abuse, mental illness, and dysfunctional relationships.

Homelessness is one of the major conditions creating the need for this ministry. Living in old cars, alleys, abandoned buildings and tent/plastic villages is often a result of substance abuse, mental disorders, personal economic crises, and/or dysfunctional relationships. Homelessness is a phenomenon relatively new to the United States, having taken root about 50 years ago. It has grown dramatically and in spite of all kinds of programs, it continues to grow.

During the Great Depression there were many men drifting from community to community looking for work while their families were lining up at government soup kitchens to be fed. They were not considered homeless, but jobless. At the same time, there was a great migration of people leaving their homes with the intention of starting a new life in other geographic areas. The majority, accustomed to rural life, lived in tents or crowded apartments and never considered themselves as homeless.

Before these last 50 years, county and federal institutions, built

---

1   Social Security Administration, Office of Beneficiary and Determination Services, *Representative Payee Program, Guide for Organizational Representative Payees, 2008* (SSA Publication No. 17-013), 7.

in the late 1800s and early 1900s, provided for the mentally ill, alcoholics, and seniors who did not have families to care for them.
There were thousands of these institutions, large and small.[2] The
police would not tolerate homelessness and transported each person
they deemed homeless to these institutions called "poor farms" and
"insane asylums." A few of these institutions were lockup facilities,
but most were left unlocked during the day. Food, clothing, and a
bunk with covers were provided. Homelessness, as we know it today, was rare.

The National Alliance to End Homelessness points out that the
seeds for homelessness were planted in the 1960s and 1970s when
these government institutions were closed, torn down, or converted
to other uses.[3] Disability checks through the SSA replaced the housing, clothing, and food that had been available in those poor farms
and insane asylums. Unfortunately, some of those receiving disability checks were not able to use the money wisely and they soon were
squandering their small income and living a homeless life.

The "Flower Children" with their counterculture lifestyle also
contributed to homelessness in that era. The rapid growth of the
drug culture was also a factor. With the closing of the institutions,
the age old presence of alcoholism, and newer substance addictions,
the development of homelessness accelerated.

Into this mix came the Vietnam War veterans. Many of them
had started using drugs available in Vietnam. Between drugs and
post traumatic syndrome a shocking number joined the ranks of the
homeless.

It is difficult to find accurate figures, but, depending on the cli-
mate, the best statistics indicate that from 1 to 1.9 percent of the
current United States population can be considered homeless today,
and the percentage is slowly growing. The estimate is that there are
3.5 million homeless in the United States.

2   "Poor House Story Home Page." History, Poor Houses by State. http://www.poor-
     housestory.com/ [accessed January 6, 2007].
3   "Homelessness in the United States." Historical Background. http://en.wikipedia.org/
     wiki/Homelessness [accessed on February 8, 2006]

According to the National Coalition for Homelessness, approximately 34 percent of the homeless population is 18 years of age and under. This group is classified as children. This means they are living in a shelter or in an area not intended for human habitation.

3.6 percent of public school children are homeless. This group increased by 26 percent from 2007 to 2008.

The homeless population is comprised of 42 percent African American, 39 percent Anglo Caucasian, 13 percent Hispanic, 4 percent Native American and 2 percent Asian. 19 percent of the homeless are victims of domestic violence. 2 percent are HIV positive. 19 percent are employed.

Approximately 875,000 homeless are veterans. The majority of the homeless veterans came from the Vietnam War, but the number of homeless veterans is growing again as some of the military personnel returning from Iraq and Afghanistan cannot adjust to life in their communities and end up on the streets.[4]

The makeup of the homeless culture is now changing due to the number of families with children who are experiencing homelessness. In Los Angeles County with a population of 9,000,000 people, there are 93,000 homeless. There are roughly 10,000 children included in this group. Children and adults living as families on the street number about 20,000 individuals.

Single parent families run up against two problems that force them from their homes and onto the streets. The first problem is the dearth of affordable housing. For several decades there was an excess of affordable housing units as families moved out of the inner city to the suburbs, but by 1999, across the United States, there was a shortage of 5.3 million affordable units.[5] This shortage continues to grow as landlords raise their rents, communities are gentrified,

---

4   The different studies made on the number and composition of the homeless segment of the population in the United States varies widely. The figures used in this book are based on the consensus of a panel discussion called "Unpacking LA" at the Signs of Hope BGU Consultation, January, 2006. A major consideration in counting the number of people who are homeless is the definition of what constitutes homelessness.
5   Affordable Housing Shrinks. "Waiting Lists Grow While Affordable Housing Shrinks." http://www.huduser.org/periodicals/rrr/html [accessed July 12, 2007].

and the government, because of limited funding, finds it harder to subsidize rents.

The second problem is low wages. By 2004 the number of people living below the poverty line in the United States had risen for the fourth straight year to 12.7 percent of the population.[6] Today, the rule of thumb is that 50,000,000 or 15 percent of the population lives below the poverty line. This rise seems to be, in part, a result of the Personal Responsibility and Work Opportunity Reconciliation Act, passed in 1996, which was created to replace some existing programs and reduce the number of people on welfare. For many it had the desired affect and forced them off the government dole and into the work force. The welfare rolls dropped precipitously. However, it needs to be remembered that declining welfare rolls simply means that fewer people are receiving government benefits. It does not mean that all of those forced off the welfare rolls are working or that all of them are receiving an adequate salary to pay for basic food, shelter, clothing, and medicine. Based on my observations, most of the salaries available to those leaving welfare or some other assistance program are minimal. It only takes one unfortunate event such as an illness or accident and the family is forced into homelessness.

There are many definitions of homelessness. There is a limited definition that resides in the minds of laypeople who notice individuals or groups of people lounging or sleeping on the streets, in the parks, or at the library, and their presence is bothersome. How they are dressed or what they are doing does not conform to the usual ideas of dress and behavior. They see young people dressed in black and draped in chains, beggars standing at off-ramps to freeways, dumpster divers picking cans out of the trash, fatigued individuals sleeping in the parks or in front of buildings, or slow moving older people pushing unsightly grocery carts with their earthly possessions. Defining homelessness in such a casual way is not helpful since some of these individuals are not homeless and are adept at

---

6   U.S. Census Bureau-Poverty. "Detailed Poverty Tables." http://www.census.gov/hhes/www/poverty/poverty.html [accessed January 8, 2008].

managing their limited income.

A more helpful definition is offered by Paul A. Rollison.[7] He categorizes and defines homeless people according to their condition as temporarily, episodically, or chronically homeless. Temporary homelessness arises when people are displaced from their usual dwellings by fires, evictions, family breakdowns, or other unexpected events. Often these people can manage their incomes and with a little help will be on their feet and housed again.

Episodically homeless people are those who frequently experience periods of being homeless. Those suffering from mental illness, living with family members, except when their disability becomes intolerable for the family, are episodically homeless. Another example is mothers escaping with their children from spousal abuse, moving in with another family, and then moving on when this family situation becomes intolerable. Often a RPO can take the managing of finances out of the middle of these points of conflict and allow better relations to develop.

The chronically homeless are those without a home for one year or more. They are more likely to suffer from mental illness and substance abuse than the other classes of homeless people. The major service of an RPO, among the homeless, is found with this group. The estimate is that 60 percent of the chronically homeless receive a disability or Title II check from the government. Also among this group are those who are on SSI but have lost contact with the SSA and others who are qualified to receive disability support but do not know how to apply. There are a few who could work and need to be in a training program.

A major contribution to chronic homelessness and joblessness is substance abuse. Individuals with an addictive nature and an inability to free themselves from this behavior can be plagued with many different contributing factors. All the causal roots are not understood, but substance abuse is extensive, destructive, and growing in the United States. Substance abuse has two important consider-

---

7   Paul A. Rollison and John T. Pardeck, *Homelessness in Rural America, Policy and Practice* (New York: The Haworth Press, Inc., 2006), 8.

ations related to the purpose of this study. First, many of those who are challenged and have an addictive personality are on disability. By law, alcoholism or drug use alone is not considered sufficient reason for a person to receive a SSI check from the SSA. There must be a dual diagnosis in which the addiction is coupled with another condition that causes an inability to hold a job. These individuals often become drug dependent as they self medicate to find relief from mental imbalance. Unfortunately, drugs and alcohol often bring a person to the point of no longer being able to work responsibly, and then they have to rely on support from SSI. The treatment centers, half way houses, room and board homes, board and care facilities, and inexpensive hotels and motels all require drug free living. Those with a chronic habit do not last long in a clean environment and become homeless.

The second consideration for those with an addictive personality is their inability to use their income support from SSI appropriately. Those working at food banks, homeless centers, Rescue Missions, medical clinics, and centers for meals, who honestly inquire into the lives of those coming for assistance, know the majority of their clients receive some kind of an assistance check, misuse it, and then access other helping services to get by until the next check is available. Sixty percent of the homeless receive a check from some government assistance program.[8]

Being mentally ill, especially with a bipolar or schizophrenic diagnosis, and without family or a friend to help monitor proper "meds" makes it almost impossible for a person with a mental disorder to manage his or her personal life. Many low income families cannot afford medications and are ill equipped to work with their young people challenged in this way. These young people are soon on the streets and disruptive.

All of those with mental disabilities are eligible to receive a SSI check. Because of their condition, they are soon required to have a Representative Payee to manage their income. If the client's disor-

---

8   Steve Lopez, "Homelessness," *Los Angeles Times,* October 19, 2005.

der is mild, having a friend or family member as the Representative Payee can work with a minimum of disagreement. Unfortunately, the stress accompanying the task is often overwhelming, and the person serving as their Representative Payee returns the check and responsibility back to the SSA. The SSA then sends the beneficiary to a RPO.

The county can assign a case worker to those who are more difficult in their behavior, but the case worker is not allowed to manage the beneficiary's income. A RPO representative has to write the checks and account for the beneficiary's income.

The most difficult task in working with those who are mentally challenged is helping them find housing. Unfortunately, the reputation of difficult and sometimes unacceptable behavior of a person goes before them; and landlords and managers of hotels, motels, room and board homes, and board and care facilities will not rent to them.

When the level of violence of an individual is too much for a local RPO to control, their SSI management can be returned to Social Security. The SSA is not equipped to manage out-of-bounds behavior, so a check is simply handed to them once a month by the receptionist.

At this point, one of two things happens to those who can become violent. One is they can be charged in court for misconduct and taken to jail or prison while it takes some years to process their case. Today almost every prison has an area or a floor reserved for those who are mentally challenged and violent, and these institutions have become major mental institutions.[9] They receive little treatment and the conditions of the prison seem to add to their violent nature.

Second, there are a few lock-up mental institutions that were not closed in the 1960s and 1970s, and these individuals become patients at these institutions. With the monitoring of "meds," their condition improves and they are released. Unfortunately, many return to their old habit of not caring for themselves and the pattern is repeated.

9   Pete Earley, *Crazy, A Father's Search Through America's Mental Health Madness* (New York: Berkley Books, 2006), 37.

The care of those with mental disorders is a national disaster.

In summary, today there are large numbers of people in the United States who, because of disability or retirement, receive an income from SSA, VA, or the welfare system. Unfortunately, many of these recipients of income from the government are homeless, struggling with substance abuse, mentally challenged, or entangled in dysfunctional relationships. The government, recognizing this problem, has created a Representative Payee program through the SSA. A part of this program calls for the development of non-profit organizations to accept those who have problems managing their incomes and working with them toward a better quality of life through careful use of these incomes.

CHAPTER 3

SOCIAL SECURITY ADMINISTRATION

A history of the Development of the SSA and RPO Program

Otto Bismark united the German Empire in 1871 and annexed Alsace-Lorraine, an industrial area that was a showpiece of the Industrial Revolution. He was a great militarist but also a brilliant politician. He saw the steady migration of families leaving the farms of Europe to work in the heavy industries of Alsace-Lorraine, realizing they would reach an age when they could no longer do this work, but would have no farm to which they could return. They would need some economic security. As Chancellor, he created the first Social Security System. "By the time America adopted social insurance in 1935 there were 34 other nations operating some form of a social insurance program."[10]

The English "Poor Laws," developed in the 1700's in Great Britain, were an acknowledgment the government had a responsibility toward the poor, but the institutions created to carry out these laws were harsh and rigid because the marginalized were branded as "undesirables." The citizens of that era generally felt it was the fault of the inmates themselves that they were in poverty and they should be made to work in order to be cared for. This system was brought by the early English settlers to the colonies. These settlers tolerated

---

10   Social Security Online History Pages. "Historical Background and Development of Social Security." http://www/socialsecurity.gov/history [accessed October 28, 2008].

some of the abusive patterns from Great Britain to be practiced in the colonies.

Not all caretakers were abusive however, and some critics wanted to improve the system. Thomas Paine (1737-1809) was the first person to propose a program of social insurance that was unique to the United States. His writings started a long, often contentious, discussion on this subject.

A Social Security program was developed for the soldiers after the War of Independence. A much more extensive Social Security program was developed for the soldiers of the Civil War. Widows of these soldiers also received benefits. Even though the soldiers and widows constituted only .6 percent of the U.S. population, as late as 1893 they were receiving $165 million or 37 percent of the federal budget.[11]

Unlike Germany, it was not so much the Industrial Revolution, but the Great Depression that triggered President Franklin D. Roosevelt to appoint a presidential committee to study the problem of economic security. As a result, the Social Security Act was signed into law in the United States on August 14, 1935. There were some provisions for the general welfare of the populace, but at the heart of the act was a social insurance program created to pay an income to retired workers, 65 years of age and older. Life expectancy was then 62.7 years. At first the income was a lump sum, but this was quickly modified to a monthly payment system.

The Post Office took on the task of providing a network of field offices for the new program, distributing applications for Social Security numbers, typing the Social Security Number cards and returning the cards to those who had applied. "35 million Social Security cards were issued through this procedure in 1936-1937."[12]

Up until 1939 only workers received benefits, but that year dependent's benefits were added for the wife and children of a worker, and survivor's benefits were added for the families of a worker who died prematurely.

---

11   Ibid.
12   Ibid.

In 1950 a major amendment raised the benefits and gave almost universal coverage.

Up until 1972, beneficiaries had to wait for a special act of Congress to receive a raise in benefits. In 1975 cost-of-living adjustments, "COLAs," were enacted and this practice continues to the present day.

On August 1, 1956, the Social Security Act was amended to cover disabled workers. At this time the SSA started to offer disability insurance and the program reached out to help the physically and mentally challenged. This amendment was the forerunner of the present Supplemental Security Income Program or SSI.

In the Social Security amendments of 1972, Congress federalized over a thousand state and local programs designed to help the disabled. These were combined into a new entity called Supplemental Security Income or SSI. This program was placed under the SSA. From that time, there have been two different departments within the SSA.

One department, called Title II, has existed from the beginning of SSA. When workers retire, their retirement income from Social Security reflects what they paid into the system. Their check comes from the Title II department.

The second department, SSI, generates checks on the basis of need. Seniors and those who are physically, mentally, emotionally, or relationally challenged, who cannot work, can find support through SSI. The Representative Payee program relates to both departments, but a RPO representative must work with each department separately.

Caring For Challenged Individuals Before SSI

During the nineteenth century in the United States, poor houses and insane asylums were developed along the same lines as found in Great Britain. In the insane asylums, because of the behavior of many of those locked up, there was always a question as to whether they were fully "human." Often there was unbelievable abuse.

Reformers worked for change in the treatment of those locked up in these facilities, but others felt the status quo was fine. Slowly, in the late 1800's and very early 1900's, as counties developed and county governments took more responsibility for their constituents, "County Poor Farms" were developed. At the same time states developed "Insane Asylums" in order to provide a lock-up situation for those too "disturbed" to be in public. Wealthier families, to avoid shame, would often lock a challenged member of their family in a room in their houses.

In the late 1930's my family lived across a county road from the Lawrence County Poor Farm in Western Pennsylvania. Several times a day we would see a police car drive up with someone who was to live at the poor farm. Some were alcoholics, others mentally challenged, and others were seniors no longer able to care for themselves. It was actually a working farm where all who were able were expected to work. Food, clothing, a bunk, and meager tobacco money were provided to each one.

Our family was empathetic toward those assigned to live there. The attitude of my parents toward those whose lives had dwindled down to that plight was influential in the shaping of my later understanding of the need for dignity and respect to be given to all persons regardless of their immediate situation, no matter how difficult and unappealing that might be.

The Great Depression triggered an awareness of senior workers who could no longer work but needed help. It wasn't until 1939, however, that government support checks began to trickle out so these older workers and spouses did not have to depend wholly on their families or savings to survive. Sometimes those who received a SSA check, but were unable to use it wisely, were also taken to the poor farm.

Caring for Challenged Individuals after SSI

In 1972, when the SSI program was created and the SSA started administrating this fund, the care of the poor, homeless, disabled, and mentally ill changed drastically. Supplying housing, food, and clothing came to an end; a monthly check was sent to recipients, and they were charged with the management of this income for their own well being.

As a result of this change, during the 1960s through the 1980s most of the County Poor Farms and Insane Asylums were closed, torn down, or converted to other uses. Only a sprinkling of institutions for the mentally ill across the United States remains today. The laws governing the confinement of those who are seriously mentally ill are vague and geographically varied. Many who are violent remain unconfined in communities.

Disability checks distributed through SSA replaced the amenities of the institutions. If a person wanted to remain in a government institution, the only way it could happen was to break the law and be locked up in a jail or prison. The rationale was that recipients receiving this support could manage their income for their own benefit. Many were able to do this or they found a friend or family member who would help.

There were four negative results of this change from institutions to checks. First, many misused their incomes on alcohol, and later on drugs as drugs became available on the streets. It is probable that through this program the United Sates government became one of the major benefactors of the illicit drug trade. No one has measured this probability, but as we work with our clients we are keenly aware of that possibility.

The second negative result was apparent in the lives of seniors who were without families, and unable to take care of themselves. Sometimes, those claiming to be helping a senior were doing little to aid the person but instead were helping themselves to the senior's money.

The third negative result was that as people were turned out of the institutions and given a monthly check, it fueled the modern homeless movement. In that same era this movement was also aided by the Flower Children, drug trade, and Vietnam veterans. More recently homelessness has been fed by those aging out of the foster care system, Iraq veterans returning home, and families with a single parent who no longer have the means to pay rent.

The homeless population continues to grow with 1 to 1.9 percent of the population in the United States currently homeless. During the 2008 election it was very sobering to see the homeless community significant enough to be considered a voting block. The State of Ohio made it possible for them to vote.

The fourth negative result was the release of the mentally ill on the streets. For those who were severely challenged, there were only a few institutions where they could be confined. Unfortunately, the laws that governed the reentry of the mentally ill person into these institutions were confusing and usually gave the decision to the one who needed treatment.

Pete Earley reports, "Seemingly overnight, states began emptying their wards and boarding up mental hospitals. Between 1960 and 1980, the number of patients in state institutions plunged from more than 500,000 to under 100,000. This massive exit was called deinstitutionalization."[13]

With the issuance of checks, it was naively anticipated these individuals would automatically find a way to manage their own resources and successfully live independently. Over the years many of these individuals struggling with mental illness have found themselves on the streets with substance abusers, challenged veterans, homeless families, etc. Many began self medicating with available street drugs which heaped more confusion into a catastrophic situation.

Jails and prisons have become the new mental institutions. Drawing the line between those in jail not mentally challenged and those with mental disabilities is difficult. It is estimated there are close to 300,000 people in jails and prisons because of their mental disabilities, making them a threat to themselves or others. Many of these people are incarcerated several years before their case is

13   Earley, 71.

heard, but eventually they are put out on the streets again. In Kern County, some of our clients come from this population.

In 1980, the SSA realized the negative affect this program was having on many beneficiaries because they could not manage their own income well. The Representative Payee Program was created to help ameliorate this situation. The purpose of the Representative Payee Program was to require those who were misusing their support income to choose a responsible family member or friend to receive their check and help them budget the use of their money. The mandated budget priorities became shelter, food, and clothing.

By 1990, the SSA realized this system worked for some challenged beneficiaries, but a large number were selecting someone who just turned over the money to them, or misused it with them. The income of seniors was often misused by their own families.

The SSA then created the Representative Payee Agency Program, later called the Organizational Representative Payee, so those who misused their income and didn't have a person of integrity to help them, were assigned to a licensed or approved organization to manage their income. Today, in all of the SSA material there is encouragement for organizations to be developed for the purpose of being a RPO.

An incentive to organize such a service is the right to charge a fee that is set by SSA. In 2010, the limit set on the fee is $37 per client each month or no more than 10 percent of the monthly income of the beneficiary. Some organizations find this fee adequate to cover their office costs, by having a closed system where clients have very little to say on the budgeting of their income. Stewards Inc employees spend more time with the clients, so fund raising is necessary to cover 20 percent of our office expenses.

The extra effort and work to create and support a caring agency that offers interaction with clients is repaid daily by the change and stability we often witness in the lives of those we serve. Andrew came to us as a referral from Social Security. His tumultuous life story illustrates some of the regeneration that can take place when order replaces chaos.

Six years ago, Andrew, a client of Stewards Inc, was living in an old but stable neighborhood of Bakersfield with his children. One evening he answered a knock at the door, and when he opened it he found himself looking down the barrel of a pistol. As he tried to slam the door, the assailant fired. The shell was deflected by his action, but still blew out his teeth on the left side of his mouth and part of his cheek. He never knew who the attacker was or why it was perpetrated.

Andrew was born in Phoenix, Arizona, one of nine children living in a two bedroom house. His mother, a person of faith, went to church. His dad, however, was an alcoholic and very contentious. One of his siblings, Charles, was deaf and could not speak, and his father "threw him away." Another brother joined a gang. But thanks to the influence of their mother, his oldest brother became a preacher. When Andrew was 11 years old, a friend of equal age taught him to smoke marijuana and together they stole wine from Andrew's father. Despite that rocky start, he completed technical school, was certified in electronics and found steady employment.

Over the years, his dysfunctional upbringing prevailed as he was in and out of jail and fathered 13 children with five different mothers. In 1988, he moved to Bakersfield, CA, with drugs and alcohol continuing to bedevil him. Finally, placed on disability, Social Security sent him to Stewards Inc in 2001. After a year, three of his children came to live with him and then the shooting happened.

Four events have now given him enough courage to stop the substance abuse and rejoice in leading a clean and sober life. First, he knows that if one of his children had opened the door he would have been shot. Second, his eldest son, while in prison, made a clock and carved the name of every family member on it. When presenting it as a gift, he asked his dad to, "Sit down and straighten up." Third, the staff at Stewards Inc believed in him and prayed for him while helping him manage his household. Fourth, he found a church home and discovered the faith of his mother.

Today, his wife of years ago is still an addict. He talks to her and prays for her, but will not become codependent. Ten of his children are doing quite well in business, their jobs, or college. While encouraging his family, Andrew remains a man of peace and joy.

CHAPTER 4

BALANCING AUTONOMY AND BENEFICENCE

Limiting the Personal Freedom of Challenged Beneficiaries

SSA and its Representative Payee Program have matured over the last couple of decades. As problems and loopholes have been identified, legislators and administrators have worked to find solutions to these problems. Consequently, the SSA programs have become more efficient.

At the community level, the biggest problem facing the SSA and RPO staffs is finding the balance between "autonomy" and "beneficence." This need is one of the major factors determining the efficiency of the program and whether the purpose of the program will be realized.

"Autonomy concerns the need to respect a person's right to self-determination and to empower a client to make the decisions that greatly affect his or her life." "Beneficence refers to the need to make decisions that are in the individual's best interest" whether they agree with the decision or not.[14]

The very nature of a Representative Payee program limits a ben-

---

14 Luchins, Daniel J., Patricia Hanrahan, Kendon J. Conrad, Courtenay Savage, Michael D. Matters, Marc Shinderman, "An Agency-Based Representative Payee Program and Improved Community Tenure of Persons With Mental Illness," *Psychiatric Services* 49 (September, 1998) 1218-1222. This article describing the study made at the University of Chicago has been a landmark study affirmed and quoted in many other articles that have called for the development of more Representative Payee Organizations.

eficiary's autonomy. This limitation is enforced when beneficiaries have abused the use of their incomes and therefore have been required to choose a Representative Payee or a RPO to help them manage their incomes. As representatives carry out their responsibilities, there are all kinds of underlying ethical judgments that have to be made. Every time a client representative sits down with the beneficiary or writes checks for their needs, the questions of what is right and what is wrong, what is helpful and what is harmful has to be answered. Even when these decisions are made with the beneficiary, the final decision is made by the representative. The beneficence of the decision may not be understood by the beneficiary, but it will be made with the best interest of the beneficiary in mind.

The need for balance between autonomy and beneficence arises throughout the program. Doctors make decisions regarding a person's disability, and then must make a second decision as to whether this person is capable of managing their Social Security income. The guidelines for making this decision are unclear. An overwhelming number of beneficiaries facing the possibility of being required to be in the Representative Payee program wish to remain autonomous. They do not want to give up the right to manage their income, and they express this vehemently to the doctor. Under this pressure, often the doctor replies, "Well, we'll let you give it a try." Is there beneficence in this decision or is the doctor giving in to save bad feelings?

This same scenario takes place when beneficiaries visit the Social Security office. Many beneficiaries request to manage their own income. The Social Security representative is faced with the question of granting their request to be autonomous in the use of their income or making a decision with beneficence and saying a beneficiary needs a representative to help them manage their income.

Usually, when the doctor's opinion is that the beneficiary is not capable of managing their income, the Social Security representative concurs with this decision. At this point, the beneficiary must present to the Social Security representative a relative or friend who will take responsibility for managing the beneficiary's money. The difficulty is the Social Security representative has no way of discerning whether this relative or friend will be ethical and make decisions with beneficence.

Even after a challenged person is assigned to a RPO, and the staff does their best to make decisions with beneficence, a disgruntled beneficiary will often return to the Social Security office to pour out frustrations about the RPO's decisions. The Social Security representative is faced with the same problem. How much autonomy should be granted? Is the RPO making decisions with beneficence?

One thing is certain; beneficence does not always elicit appreciation. Most beneficiaries want a source of income that is unencumbered with any kind of guiding principles or other's opinions. They want to be totally autonomous.

When the reasons are enumerated as to why individuals who are receiving SSA, SSI, or VA support must be part of the Representative Payee Program, it is understandable why they cannot have complete autonomy. The major reason is substance abuse or an addiction coupled with mental illness, such as schizophrenia or bi-polar disorder. Other reasons are frequent hospitalization, homelessness, lack of financial skills, and impulsive spending that leaves no funds for the basics of food, shelter, and clothing.

There are two points at which SSA needs to tighten up its regulations. First, many of the beneficiaries who need to be in the program fall through the cracks. In 2006, of the 49,122,624 in the United States receiving disability or retirement checks, there were 5,134,004 required to be in the Social Security Representative Payee Program, either with a personal Representative Payee or in a RPO. It is estimated this figure is about 50 percent of those who should be in the program. This estimation has not been verified by a study, but it is an obvious fact to any person working with marginalized people. There is a common knowledge among marginalized people about how to evade being put in this SSA program. SSA needs to work more closely with other agencies, so when these individuals in need of guidance are identified, they are put in the program.

Second, SSA should not allow beneficiaries assigned to the Representative Payee Program to change Representative Payees or RPOs so often. Anecdotal evidence demonstrates when people are into substance abuse they do not want controls on their incomes and will argue and scream to get out of the system so they can control their income. Some beneficiaries will go back to the Social Security office over and over until, unfortunately, they find a Social Security representative who will release them from the Representative Payee program. Like a child throwing a tantrum, when the SSA representative holds firm with former decisions, the beneficiary usually settles down and life does get better.

All decisions for a beneficiary are recorded and available in the computer at each person's desk in the Social Security office. Every time the beneficiary visits the Social Security office, it is recorded. If the Social Security staff would use the record of visits and decisions and be consistent in their decisions, it would be more beneficial to the client.

A study by the University of Chicago revealed, "the most important finding was the more than nine fold reduction in the number of days clients spent in the state hospital-from a mean of 68 days to seven days-in the year after enrollment in the Representative Payee Program, with a parallel reduction in the number of days in state and private (Medicaid funded) hospitals, from 97 to 15 days. The number of hospitalizations also decreased. These findings suggest that the Representative Payee Program was quite successful in maintaining clients in the community."[15]

The identification of more beneficiaries of Social Security income who need help in managing their income, mandating their being in the Representative Payee program, and not allowing them to habitually change their Representative Payee are needed to help each one realize a better life. Even though only a few will be totally rehabilitated, almost all will live a life that is better than the

---

15   Ibid.

life they are now living.

The story of Monique's struggle with life illustrates some of the advantages that come from relationships that maintain that balance between autonomy and beneficence.

Monique was born 37 years ago, a preemie, in Dennison, Texas. By the time the doctor said she was strong enough to go home, her mother had disappeared and abandoned her daughter. Fortunately, the grandfather was there to take her home and care for her.

In those early years she realized she was one of five siblings who shared the same absentee mother but all had different fathers. As a consequence, Monique was shuttled back and forth between Foster Care Homes and being raised by her grandfather.

She stayed clear of drugs in her teen years, but could not stay clear of two uncles who sexually abused her and an aunt who beat her. She remembers her will being so strong that she would not cry.

In her 20's she found herself divorced and living in Ridgecrest, CA, with a son and a daughter. Her life was so broken she finally gave into using drugs and soon the drugs dominated her life. As so often happens, she grew up being abused and became an abuser. She couldn't stop abusing her children even though she knew how wrong it was. Once she had to call Child Protective Services to keep from hurting them. Another time she choked her son so severely he lost consciousness. To keep her children from her own destructive behavior, she called Child Protective Services a second time and asked for the kids be taken from her.

Eventually she found herself in Bakersfield, CA, and at her worst moment, two good things happened to her. First, Stewards Inc became her Representative Payee with Robbie Sutton becoming her friend and Client Representative in the office.

Second, she met a man, 13 years her senior, who loved her and believed in her unconditionally. He took Monique in to live with him even though she was still on drugs.

Between Robbie at Stewards Inc and the man she eventually married, the will to live a better life began to take hold. One day it dawned on her that her persistent drug use was wearing her husband down and destroying their relationship which she so valued. She did not want this to happen. This became the boost she needed to reform her ways.

Remaining clean and sober became a battle. Sometimes she became angry and would not speak to her husband for weeks. She knew she deeply loved him, but still carried a great deal of anger. He remained unconditionally devoted to her. There were times when she wanted to walk away from it all, but he wouldn't let her. During those times she kept thinking of her wedding vow, "till death do us part" and she clung to the permanency of her marriage.

She describes how it felt to have someone like Robbie at Stewards Inc take control and manage her income. "To have someone else manage your income makes you feel helpless and like nothing at first. However, when that person in control of your money calls you by name, listens to you, and makes suggestions about how to live better, it gives you strength inside to try harder to do better."

Forgiveness has been a part of her recovery. She confronted her uncles about their abuse and then forgave them. She has forgiven her mother as well.

After marrying and raising her two children and two of her husband's children, Monique had some leisure time and began to slip back into some of her old habits. She knew she needed to be busy so she decided to go back to school. With her husband's support, she is studying at Santa Barbara Business College. She has learned two things about herself at school. First, she can get A's. Second, she is a leader.

Monique shared recently that she had been diagnosed with stomach cancer. When asked how she was feeling about the news, she said, "I learned long ago not to let anything take the harmony out of my relationships or peace out of my life. I am taking time to smell the roses. If there is something to be feared, face it straight on and it will become smaller as you understand it."

How does someone graciously emerge from the chaos of life

and tailor her attitudes in order to have confidence and courage to face the future? The catchy title of a book written by Dr. Eugene C. Rollins, *Grace Is Not A Blue-Eyed Blonde,* tips us off.[16] Its text reminds us that the understanding and embracing of grace needs to permeate every layer of life in order to live successfully. The grace that flows from our creator to and through us is an undeserved gift. Grace is not passive, but active and when accepted, is freeing and redemptive.

We pray for that grace to flow through every decision we make on behalf of each beneficiary.

---

16 Eugene C. Rollins, *Grace Is Not A Blue-Eyed Blonde* (Bloomington: Authorhouse, 2008).

CHAPTER **5**

EXPECTATIONS AND RESULTS OF THIS FAITH-BASED PROGRAM

Anticipated Outcomes in the Lives of Beneficiaries and their Communities

Everyone loves a success story. It seems to be part of the American culture. Hollywood has taught us that happy endings are meant to follow the unthinkable tragic events that are a part of life. We need to be able to make meaning out of the pitfalls that beset most of us.

When telling the story of Stewards Inc, we are frequently asked, "Do you have any successes?" That is a landmine question akin to, "When did you stop beating your wife?" One runs the risk of being misunderstood no matter how you answer. The person who asks usually gets tired of waiting for a crisp definitive answer as we hem and haw about needing to define success so we can talk about the subject.

We do need to explore the expectations and real results of this faith-based program. The reasons for involvement in this government program are compelling; the anticipated results in the lives of those affected can be life changing and the responsibilities we assume for the SSA are mandatory.

Can we expect to have measurable success?

A for-profit enterprise has sharp measurements to define success, and most of those have to do with a healthy bottom line. A non-profit faith motivated enterprise also has to have a healthy bottom line or there is no mission. However, the real measurement of success comes in lives renewed, despair exchanged for confidence, addictions brought under control, mental illness symptoms alleviated with proper medication, family violence turned into control and tenderness, children united with parents and perhaps the main issue; people facing life issues with their hope rekindled.

Measurement marks:

Are those involved better able to experience a more abundant life because they have been helped with budgeting and managing their Social Security income in order to have an adequate living space and food for their family?

Have the beneficiaries of this faith-based program experienced hope and support for a better future because the staff has been available and able to pray with them, at their request, in times of need and crisis?

Are those with substance abuse problems leading more stable lives because we have managed their assets?

Are those with mental health issues better able to maintain on their medications because of our support and encouragement?

This is not an exhaustive list of expectations, but it does begin to outline the signposts of success which are relative to each life and each situation. Success is a dynamic and moving target that is determined by where the life of each beneficiary and our ministry intersect.

The story of Darlene illustrates this. If one were to sit down with her today, the thought would be, "Here is a woman who has lived her years in peace and orderliness." However, the dramatic back story reveals both trauma and victory.

Darlene was born 45 years ago in Oklahoma. The Hippie Movement, as it was popularly known, was sweeping the country and was the lifestyle in which her parents were enmeshed. She knows very little about her father and mother since they gave her to her aunts and uncles to raise when she was only two years old, in order to pursue their own freedoms. Her father died when she was four and her mother, still chasing life, was married seven times in the ensuing years.

The relatives who were charged with Darlene's childhood were living out the same experimental model of life. She was often used as their entertainment when as a toddler they gave her alcohol so they could watch and laugh at her inebriated antics. By the time she was five years old, the caretakers taught her to use marijuana and at nine they gave her speed. Using and drinking was part of their lifestyle and by the time the entertainment factor wore off, Darlene was enmeshed in the same destructive patterns to which she had been abusively exposed.

This mode of life meant doing as she wanted without any thought or knowledge of the consequences. Free love meant random partners without commitment. Drugs and alcohol became a right and an increasing pressure. She had no home, only cheap housing as her extended family drifted from place to place.

Thirty years ago, on her fifteenth birthday, she married and soon delivered a son whom she named Glenn. She mothered him and loved him, but the wanton lifestyle continued. Often she contemplated suicide, but the thought of leaving her son to the care of her family and friends called her back to being a mother.

When Glenn became 18, and searching for a better life, he joined the Navy. At this point, Darlene became a beneficiary of Social Security and was referred to Stewards Inc. For the first few years as our client, her life bumped up and down along the same paths. Our staff tried everything in their collective experience to bring change to her life, but nothing seemed to work. We were able to keep her housed and fed, but drugs and alcohol kept flooding through her life.

Three years ago, Glenn announced he was coming home from the service. This was the breakthrough, an event that was worth a lifestyle change, suggested our client representative. It did not bring about an immediate change in her behavior, of course. Darlene has a lot of work to do to overcome a lifetime of abuse, however she began to make her apartment a little more presentable and her life slowly began to improve.

Glenn came home after 10 years in the Navy where everything had been "shipshape." Even with his help it took over two years for Darlene to become clean and sober. She found hope for the future through the faithfulness of her son, our staff's encouragement and mentoring of two Christian fellowships.

On Saturday evenings she attends a candlelight service at a local Nazarene church where she says, "The pastor's warm voice and clear message speaks to my needs and strengthens my faith." On Sunday morning she attends "Set Free," a biker's church group where she enjoys the music and worship.

It has been a long journey of many years, but now Darlene is a woman with her life in good order. She has a faith that brings a plan and hope for the future.

Hopelessness, or the inability to sense there is an attainable future, is endemic in both the communities of the marginalized and in the individuals themselves. Stewards Inc believes that our deepest calling is to bring hope to the communities and to the individuals. In our view, that hope is found in God through Jesus Christ. But our call is not to persuade those under our care to share that belief only because we promote or suggest it. Our call is to be the servers of those who come to us for help so they might evidence God's grace in action, and by their choice be the recipients of that gift in their own lives. The Bible is clear in its message that God has a way to bring people to be "right with Him." That plan is not to make people rich or successful or famous, but to bring hope for the future.

We seek to recognize the worth of each person as a creation of God and to treat them with the dignity they deserve. We are available to pray with clients, at their request, in times of need and crisis and try to connect them to caring churches and groups that can further their journey toward an abundant life.

Not all RPOs are faith-based or share this conviction. Among the faith-based RPOs and secular RPOs there are for-profit and non-profit organizations. Those that are for-profit are usually part of a for-profit business such as a residential care facility. The purpose of all of these organizations is to provide a sound financial and budgeting counsel service that ensures shelter, food, and clothing for the beneficiary from his monthly Social Security income. Some of these organizations provide case workers who go to the homes of their clients to monitor their well-being and help them overcome life problems in an appropriate way. All of these services, when properly managed, provide valuable help to challenged individuals and their communities.

Another success story for Stewards Inc is a deep satisfaction for all of us who work and volunteer with this organization because we know that we make a difference in individual lives every day. We share the pleasure of working together as a team toward goals that even though elusive, do break through and are attained on a regular basis. The task, however, can be wildly frustrating and anyone involved has days of just wanting to "throw in the towel" and leave the mess of other's lives and well-being to the Lord.

Social Security Administration Expectations (Outcomes)

Accepting the responsibility of acting on behalf of the SSA, by using their program, also brings very measurable mandates for being in compliance with the guidelines for being recognized as an approved RPO.

There are specific "outcomes" expected by the SSA:

1. The first outcome to which all RPOs are committed is seeing that every beneficiary is adequately housed. The SSA states that housing is the first priority. Often a beneficiary has been living in dumpsters, abandoned buildings, in a makeshift tent, or under the stars. It is not easy to coax them into staying in an apartment, a motel room or a care facility.

Seniors are frequently in abusive living situations with family or friends. They love their housemates, hope and pray they will stop their abusiveness, and do not want to leave them. Sometimes, when a RPO takes control of the income of the senior, the situation becomes tolerable. However, if the client is being neglected, he/she may need to be moved to an appropriate place or level of care.

There are other good incidents when the family or a friend takes a beneficiary into their home and an agreed upon budget is worked out for rent, utilities and other expenses so the payment can be guaranteed by the RPO. This sort of living arrangement can be beneficial to all involved.

Part of finding appropriate housing necessitates the assessment of the physical and mental well-being of the individual. Perhaps this person needs to be in a room and board, board and care, assisted living, or nursing home situation. Sometimes a proper determination can be made by the RPO staff, but often it takes professional help.

Legally, a person cannot be forced to stay where they do not want to live. The representative from the RPO has to be persuasive but cannot be forceful. Of the 1,600 beneficiaries of Stewards Inc, only fewer than five cannot be persuaded to sleep inside instead of under a bridge or behind bushes.

2. The second outcome to which all RPOs are committed is the creation of a budget for each individual that will make it possible for the beneficiary to have food all month. The majority of our beneficiaries receive a check for food each Monday morning. Those who cannot come to the office can have their check mailed to them.

If a beneficiary habitually misuses this grocery money for things other than food, the check is made out to a cooperating grocery store instead of to them personally with a memo of "food only" noted. For those struggling with substance abuse, the weekly check can be divided and handed out twice a week. In case of a severe problem, a small daily check is made out to a grocery store for food only.

3. The third outcome is to budget the beneficiaries' income so necessary clothing and other personal care items can be purchased.

Checks are usually made out to specific stores with a description of the items to be purchased in the check memo. Receipts returned to us are required for all purchases of this nature. If the beneficiary saves for a larger purchase, they are required to obtain, in writing, the price of the item, plus tax. A check is made out for that amount to the store.

4. Some RPOs only budget for shelter, food, and clothing, but Stewards Inc includes a fourth outcome when possible. This might be defined as a healthier physical, emotional, relational status of the client. When new beneficiaries come to Stewards Inc, they are asked to bring all of their bills. Sometimes a whole box of due and past due bills will be presented to be sorted out. The purpose is to protect merchants who are owed for legitimate merchandise and services and to help put the beneficiary's life in order. Utility bills, credit card bills and fines usually turn up and payment arrangements need to be made. The policy of Stewards Inc is to pay cable TV and telephone bills if the bills are not excessive. Our goal is to mainstream each person back into the community as an accepted and respected individual.

When new beneficiaries arrive at the office, they usually have been referred to us because their life patterns are destructive to their well-being. The representative taking down their information has to assess habits and conditions without violating the privacy to which the individual is entitled.

One desired result of the income control is a reduction in drug use. By directly paying for rent, groceries, clothing, and personal needs, less disposable money is available for illegal drugs. Positive reinforcement for a more productive life comes from directing those who are struggling with this issue into sober and drug free housing situations along with linkage to Al Anon and other support groups.

Those who have the most difficulty maintaining a reasonable lifestyle are individuals who often have a dual diagnosis. They suffer from a mental illness and also are self-medicating with illegal drugs or alcohol for a remedy and some relief.

Community Expectations and Benefits

Stewards Inc not only works and plans for improvement in the lives of its beneficiaries, but also for the betterment of the larger community in which it operates.

The first community benefit is the reduction of the number of challenged individuals sleeping in front of stores, in the alleys or pitching tents on empty lots. 60 percent of those who seem to be homeless actually already receive SSA, SSI, or VA checks. If these individuals land in a hospital or jail they are identified as receiving income from the government through any source. Their income can then be held by the SSA until they sign up with a RPO. When all this happens, the responsible organization's first job is to coax them into appropriate housing. This becomes a benefit and desirable outcome for both the community and the individual.

There are at least two categories of individuals that need to be identified and helped. Many of the city and county agencies work together on this problem, as well as non-profit ministries. First, there are the severely mentally ill folks who have been granted SSI support, but have lost contact with the SSA and their income, but are not capable of reconnecting and establishing a routine to work within the system. As an RPO, Stewards Inc helps them reconnect through a local Social Security office when they become clients, and monitors that the funds are used wisely for their well-being by acting as their Representative Payee.

Second, are the homeless individuals who are too challenged to hold employment and literally have no income. We can facilitate a doctor's evaluation to determine they are indeed disabled and unable to work. When helped to complete the proper forms and paperwork at the local Social Security office in order to apply for SSI support, we can begin to get these folks into a more stable life mode. This process can take up to a year to complete.

The third community benefit comes from the SSA, SSI and VA income being curtailed from going into the illegal economy and drugs. Both housed and homeless recipients are capable of using their money for drug use. There are many conflicting studies on the percentage of those who use their income in this way.

When beneficiaries are assigned to a RPO, something traumatic has caused a Social Security representative to make this mandatory call. We cannot ask why a new client has been referred to us, but we know there are usually drugs involved, and always a misuse of their income in some way. If the new beneficiary is homeless, the RPO representative will assume drugs are involved.

Of the 1,600 beneficiaries assigned to Stewards Inc, the best we can estimate is about 900 to 1,200 were homeless or would be home-less without having the help of mandatory discipline in managing their income. Knowing that almost all homeless adults use drugs and using criteria from University of Chicago studies, it would seem that Stewards Inc had the opportunity of keeping $9,700,000 from going into the drug trade in Kern County in 2009. This is not money that is withheld and kept somewhere else, but has been utilized in-stead by the checks written for rents, groceries, utilities, clothes, etc. for the benefit of the individual client. In this way the decisions for how the funds are dispersed are controlled and the money is kept from the illegitimate economy and put in the legitimate economy of the community. By working with over a thousand landlords and other business people in the community, Stewards Inc makes a sig-nificant difference.

A fourth outcome and benefit for a community is the reduction of taxes being used for hospitalization and incarceration of the home-less. Housing definitely affects the quality of life of beneficiaries and reduces hospital and jail time. All studies agree that adequate housing cuts approximately 56 days per year from the time a home-less person would normally spend in a hospital or jail.[17] Putting these studies together with our experience at Stewards Inc, taking into account this area's mild weather, and by carefully managing the income of our beneficiaries, a fair estimate would be that Stewards

---

17 Luchins, D. J., P. Hanrahan, K. J. Conrad, C. Savage, M. D. Matters, M. Shinderman, "An agency-based representative payee program and improved community tenure of persons with mental illness." (Sept., 1998) 49 (9): 1218-22.

Inc saved Kern County around $22,400,000 in hospitalization and incarceration costs in 2009. There is no way to factor in the savings through the reduction of police, ambulance, and fire department emergency calls.

Another community outcome is the refurbishing of low income housing that is facilitated because the landlords have a dependable cash flow from the tenants whose rents are paid directly from their income. A major complaint of landlords managing older hotels, motels, and houses is that low income individuals and families often will not pay their rent, will not move when they are in arrears, and are often destructive of the property. When a RPO manages a beneficiary's income, the RPO can guarantee that the rent will be paid and if the property is damaged, the landlord will be compensated. When there is more than one beneficiary in the same hotel or motel, the RPO has leverage to ask the building be fixed up and the rent levels be kept at a reasonable rate.

After 13 years of serving challenged people in Bakersfield, CA, there are now 111 beneficiaries of Stewards Inc living in the six downtown hotels. Every one of these hotels has been refurbished. Many of the motels that charge a monthly rent have also been painted and renewed. Landlords and managers, with rooms and apartments to rent, come by our office continuously and ask if we have anyone looking for a rental, or if they can post an advertisement on our bulletin board.

Beneficiaries tend to move around a lot. Two office policies help keep this at a minimum. First, Social Security requires a rental agreement for everyone living in an apartment or house. Stewards Inc extends this policy to every living situation since it is a tangible agreement that tends to maintain better relationships and longer term tenancy. The second office policy is the beneficiaries inspect and select their own housing. If the Stewards Inc representative selects the housing for a person, the beneficiary will complain and blame the problems and the choice on the representative. The exception is if someone needs a higher level of care, we actively choose the best situation for them.

Is it all worth the effort? Is the effort a success? Are people's lives impacted for the better? Are most of the people we serve happy we are in their lives? Does our faith based ministry help the community as well as the individual clients? One can resoundingly give a positive response to all those questions.

Do we do this perfectly? Is everyone we serve happy to have us controlling their income? Do we do everything right? Are we always wise in our counsel?

Those discomforting questions require a reverberating negative.

We are truly grateful God does not expect us to be perfect to be successful. In fact, God tells us blatantly that none of us are even acceptable without the receiving of the gifts of His truth and grace. God just asks us to be available, teachable and faithful.

—

CHAPTER 6

LEADERSHIP

Identifying Traits Needed for Successful Leadership

Ministry opportunities phase in and phase out over the decades. Effective ministry models successfully used in one era can become relics in another. Societies change and those of faith who want to emulate the ministries Christ encouraged two thousand years ago must thoughtfully discover how they can be embodied in a new way today.

With the growing marginalized block of impoverished people in the United States, and the new openness of the government to work with faith groups to meet the needs of this population, there is an unprecedented opportunity for the church. Because poverty, homelessness, substance abuse, and mental illness is endemic in every community in the United States and the SSA is present in every community, the church can be a catalyst for change in new ways by using the SSA RPO program to more effectively use government support to ameliorate the lives of these people.

RPOs need to be planted in every town and city across the United States by evangelical Christians. It is not that the problems facing the marginalized community are all spiritual, but the underlying basis of many of the problems are so deeply entrenched in people's lives, it takes more than good income management to revitalize their life structure. A person may have government support through the SSA, the latest psychotropic drugs, low income housing, and helpful case workers; but because of the depth of the problems and needs of some individuals, real change happens only by acceptance of personal redemption – received by faith - through Christ, who brings hope, peace, and joy.

Robbie Sutton, one of the Stewards Inc client representatives, tells this story.

On a cool, overcast day in November 2006, Julia, a tall attractive woman with a radiant smile came into Stewards Inc. Her face was glowing, eyes sparkling, seemingly indicative of a worry-free life of leisure. The reality of her story, however, revealed to the contrary.

Julia came into our office to sign up for payee services in order to receive her government disability support from Social Security. She had just finished serving a term of seven years in the California State Prison System. As a matter of fact, she had been in a revolving door of being in and out of prison for the past 18 years.

The second child born into a family with too many children, Julia ran away from home at a young age. To survive on the streets, she became involved in crime and substance abuse. As she matured, she became pregnant and gave birth to a beautiful baby girl. Her addictions and lifestyle prohibited her from being able to care for this baby, so she gave her away for someone else to raise. She continued to long for her baby, to experience being a mother, and to be present for her child. But that was only a dream. In real life Julia continued on the road to destruction going in and out of prison. That is until November 2006.

As a new client she was assigned to me for intake. She told me, "I made a choice when I was released this time, I'm changing my life." I was impressed with her spunky fortitude and I determined to be an encourager for her life as well as working as her payee helping with a budget and money matters. She entered a faith-based sober living home where she gave her heart and life to God and began to blossom.

Julia discovered many gifts she had never known she had. "I learned how to survive in an honest way," she said. Only a few months later, she regained custody of her beautiful daughter, now 13 years old. Julia and her child moved into their own place that they could call home.

Two years later, Julia became her own payee and moved away from California. She dropped into the office to say, "Goodbye, it gave me hope and thanks so much for believing in me." She has since reunited with the father of her daughter and they live together as a family. "I still have struggles every day, and I have learned that I can't take anything for granted…I owe it all to God." She said.

Julia's parting advice to others? "Don't ever give up on yourself!"

This chapter is less about leadership in general than about the kind of leadership God can use to change lives through a RPO. In presenting this program, one might think the ministry is one dimensional, directed only to the beneficiaries of Social Security, but the door is also wide open for a good leader to be salt and light to the staff, volunteers, and community who support the ministry.

During the thirteen years my staff and I have been developing this ministry, we have watched four RPOs fail. Two of them were faith-based and two of them were secular. All of them failed through flawed leadership and not a lack of clients. By looking briefly at the four that failed, one can discover four qualities that need to be part of a leader's character for the ministry to succeed.

Some years ago I needed advice on how to respond to certain clients who were so mentally ill that they could not comprehend budgeting. They were always pressuring our office to give them all of their month's income immediately after its deposit. I went to a Christian organization and asked the director, in a rather light hearted way, to reveal the tricks of the trade to me so I would know how to respond to the clients. She had only one answer. Slamming her fist on her desk four times, she yelled, "you gotta be tough, tough, tough, tough. That is what I tell my staff!" I carefully backed out of the conversation and the office. The old truism that "ministry without compassion can turn brutal," became apparent in that office. She was later transferred from her responsibilities, and the RPO where we met when she dispensed her advice continued to decline after she was transferred.

Contrary to her advice, a leader in this kind of ministry must have compassion and lead the staff and those who support them in being compassionate. The compassion is more critical than empathy. It enables being profoundly prompted or moved to appropriate action by the pain and condition of others.

Because of the nature of the ministry in a RPO, unconditional compassion becomes the basis for the ethics and morality of the individual client representative who cares for the beneficiary. Compassion guides the representative who has power over the life of the beneficiary to treat each one with dignity and embrace the struggle to insert hope back into their life. No matter how disgusting the smell, appearance, or language, compassion can make it possible to work with all beneficiaries for their well-being.

At the heart of God's creation there is a goodness; grace, mercy, and comfort. God's presence runs like a stream through humanity. At times that stream is flooded by a torrent and is difficult to detect, but when the flood recedes, the stream is there and still flowing. Many of our clients lives are at flood stage when they come to us; the stream is hard to detect, but it is ever flowing.

Appropriate compassion also enables the client representatives to maintain boundaries for themselves, so the beneficiaries do not become dependent on them. It is easy for compassion to override judgment and create a dependency situation. This pitfall is one of the reasons at Stewards Inc we maintain an open office without any walls, so the representatives can overhear the conversations around them. If a representative is creating a dependency situation, and another representative hears the conversation, it is considered appropriate to mention it.

One of the hazards of this ministry is Secondary Traumatic Stress

Disorder, commonly called compassion fatigue or burnout:

Studies confirm that caregivers play host to a high level of compassion fatigue. Day in, day out, workers struggle to function in care giving environments that constantly present heart wrenching, emotional challenges. Affecting positive change in society, a mission so vital to those passionate about caring for others, is perceived as elusive, if not impossible. This painful reality, coupled with first-hand knowledge of society's flagrant disregard for the safety and well being of the feeble and frail, takes its toll on everyone from full time employees to part time volunteers. Eventually, negative attitudes prevail.[18]

This disorder is more than just a possibility in this ministry. It is a probability that it will occur to workers if there is not a good and consistent program to combat it. Our program is regular training group discussions and prayer.

Before starting Stewards Inc, as told in Chapter 1, when I volunteered to paint and repair the offices of an agency that was a RPO. Everyone working in the office was a volunteer and enjoyed what they were doing, but no one was in charge of organizing the systems and paper work to insure a smooth running office. They had 67 clients. Slowly over the months, as the office became more and more disorganized, they lost track of how much money belonged to each client that was being held in a common account. Finally the local Social Security Director stepped in and shut them down.

From that experience I learned that leaders in a ministry of this type must value organization. They need to be willing to spend time developing in-house office systems and methods of interfacing with the community that insure the realization of its stated goals. There are seven different areas of relationship that need to have interfacing systems for the ministry to run smoothly:

1. The staff who carries the daily work and interacts with the beneficiaries.
2. The beneficiaries who are asked to place trust for their well-

---

18   Compassion Fatigue Awareness Project. http://www.compassionfatique.org [accessed September 3, 2008].

being in this organization.
3. The local Social Security office that determines how much each beneficiary receives month by month.
4. The bank and its program that safeguards the money as it flows from Social Security through the organization and out into the community's businesses.
5. The hundreds of landlords and businesses that serve the organization's beneficiaries in the community.
6. The courts and prisons that, too frequently, become a reality in the life of a beneficiary.
7. The health care system, including mental health agencies, with whom an organization needs to partner to care for beneficiaries.

All of these entities can be linked together for the benefit of the beneficiaries through a well run RPO.

The development of clear job descriptions for each staff member is a priority for the leader in order to keep all the systems functioning. A description of the authority that accompanies each job responsibility and the lines of communication for which they are responsible need to be included.

The ministry that is disorganized or poorly organized will be limited in the accomplishment of its purpose. Because of the sheer difficulty of managing this challenged population, both the ministry and business components of the organization will collapse when the systems and job descriptions are not in place as the number of beneficiaries escalates.

There are many different types of business systems on the market, but none that is written for a RPO. *The AMA Handbook of Project Management* gives the basics for arriving at the point of having systems and job descriptions that will help a leader realize the purpose of the ministry.[19] But the leader must take time to write out the unique systems and job descriptions required for a well run office.

---

19   Paul C. Dinsmore and Jeannette Casbanis-Brewin, *The AMA Handbook of Project Management* (New York: Amacombooks, 2006).

Several years ago, while waiting for some checks, I was sitting outside of the Director's office at the local Social Security office. Suddenly, a local businessman, who was obviously quite upset, rushed past me and, without knocking, pushed into the Director's office. I watched as he threw a large stack of checks on her desk. He angrily explained that the manager of the RPO next to his market had asked him to keep honoring her beneficiaries' checks since the beneficiaries needed food and, not to worry, the checks would be covered. He continued to accept the checks until he received his bank statement and realized the checks were worthless. The overdraft charge on the checks returned for insufficient funds was close to a thousand dollars.

Two days later, I received a call from the Social Security Director asking if our organization could take over three hundred clients from that RPO. We accepted, even though we knew we would have to deal with a lot of disgruntled beneficiaries and landlords.

The next morning in the newspaper was a muddled story of how the RPO had been closed because of a misuse of funds.

The clear message of this story is that a leader must be a trustworthy person of integrity. This quality needs to be an innate part of the leader's nature, if it is going to be an innate part of the staff. "Without honesty, the bottom drops out of all other virtues. Love is acclaimed the supreme quality of the Christian life, but Paul, who says that of faith, hope, and love, the greatest is love, also declares that love must be without hypocrisy (cf. "Your love must be genuine" [Rom. 12:9 RSV]).[20]

In the Gospel of John, Nathanael received one of the highest compliments that can be given a person, and it came from Jesus when he said, "Here is a true Israelite; no deceit in him."[21] This scripture is an echo of the Psalmist saying, "How happy is the man the Lord does not charge with sin and in whose Spirit is no deceit."[22]

Stewards Inc pays $15,500 a year for insurance, and the major-

---

20 The Interpreter's Bible, Vol. 12, (New York: Abington Press, 1957) 69.
21 John 1:47 (Christian Standard Bible).
22 Psalm 32:2 (Christian Standard Bible).

ity of that money is protection against fraud. The insurance is not to stop the possibility of fraud, but is designed to cover the lost funds in case fraud happens. The only true insurance against fraud is integrity in the heart and mind of the director and staff.

A young woman who had been working outside of her home wanted to work from home to be with her children. She decided to start a RPO. Her idea was that if the clients did not know the location of her house, all business could be conducted over the telephone and through the mail system. As I was helping her set up the business, she declared she was going to try and turn this business into a money maker and had dreams of making it big. About six months later she called and asked if Stewards Inc could take on her twenty-seven clients.

A leader in this ministry needs to be incarnational in purpose. If he or she seeks power, ego strokes, money, or success, this work is not for them. The bottom line is when a person works with those who are marginalized in the community, it marginalizes him or her as well. The greatest example of this in all of Christendom is the ministry of Christ. He lived and worked with the outcasts and misfits and allowed himself to be typecast and criticized in order to conduct his ministry.

The jaw dropping life story of the homeless man, told in chapter 8 of the Gospel of Luke underlined what healing and redemption can mean to the individual and how the ones involved get caught in the backlash. A naked, mentally ill man living in a cave has his life transformed and is sent away to tell others about what God can do to redeem life. The community is so frightened by what happened that they beg Jesus and his followers to go away and leave them alone.[23]

Stewards Inc manages millions of dollars for marginalized people. Every once in a while a person will suggest a way that the ministry could become a money maker, or that our office systems could be copyrighted to create income. This kind of long range plan-

23 Luke 8: 26-37 (New Living Translation).

ning can be tempting, but is not the real measurement of successful Christian leadership. The long range planning of a leader needs to design ways to fulfill the purpose for which the ministry was created.

When Paul came by ship to Ephesus, on his way to Jerusalem, he called the leaders of the church to be with him. After sharing many things, for a summary statement, he used the words of Christ and said, "It is more blessed to give than to receive."[24] This blessing must describe the heart of the person who desires to lead a RPO.

Every gift and quality of leadership is worthy and usable in ministry when given back to God with a humble spirit for use to his glory. For a RPO to fulfill its purpose, its leaders must have the gifts of compassion, organization, integrity, and possess a generous spirit.

---

24   Acts 20:35 (Christian Standard Bible).

CHAPTER 7

THEOLOGICAL AND BIBLICAL BASE FOR THIS MINISTRY

Exploring the Christian Motivation for Developing this Ministry

A solid theology and Biblical base of understanding must be the undergirding for tackling this secular service to reconstruct it into a ministry that builds bridges of hope for marginalized persons away from dead end life styles to a more sustainable future.

Jeremiah watched his nation be desecrated and the people pushed to despair through battle and rebellion to the point where he looked around and wrote, "This whole land shall become a ruin and a waste."[25]

Ruin and waste come in many forms. Every day as I watch the parade of beneficiaries coming to the Stewards Inc office with questions or to pick up a check, I see folks like Mary, tall and emaciated, with her black hood and unkempt black hair, wandering slowly through the office. It never crosses her mind to sign in, to differentiate between waiting area and work area, or to understand that she is quietly chattering to herself in a one way conversation. She wanders around until a staff member hands her a daily food check made out to a market and suggests she go get something to eat.

---

25   Jer. 25:11 (NRSV).

Another frequent visitor, Bradley, comes in several times each day and asks for the telephone book that the staff has put aside for his personal use. His clothes are so dirty they are slick. He smells so bad you wonder how much his nose can take. His compulsion to slurp water is so strong that we have to ask him to abandon the drinking fountain after awhile so others can also have a drink. He tears a few pages out of his book, hands it back, and goes out the door.

A longtime client, Lois, has become volatile and abusive and her demeanor is deteriorating. In the office, on the street, and wherever she lives, she is disruptive. Reasoning with her is impossible. Only the presence of the police can settle her down.

These people are living, walking examples of ruin and waste. Jeremiah spoke to the ruin and waste of his day and built that bridge of hope when he said, "For surely I know the plans I have for you, says the Lord, plans for your welfare and not for harm, to give you a future of hope."[26] These same words speak the truth of God's care and promise today as a bridge of hope to Mary, Bradley, and Lois, as well as to those places and people who are living in dead ends of ruin and waste in our own communities.

The beauty of Jeremiah's words is that they unveil a mind that did not give in to despair as the prophet looked at the ruin and waste of the land. He did not doubt God wills good, or that future good is possible. He saw hope. Likewise, as Stewards Inc staff, as we look at a thousand other lives alongside Mary, Bradley, and Lois, we do not despair. At the heart of our hope is God's desire for the best for his creation, for his best for our beneficiaries.

On the surface, day by day, in the Steward Inc office and on the streets, our staff hopes our clients, who are living out irrational lives because of mental illness and chemical imbalance, will find a measure of stability and a rhythm to their lives that will enable them to find contentment and a more abundant life. Sometimes it happens, but more often it does not.

---

26 Jer. 29:11 (NRSV).

The writer of Proverbs wrestled with unfulfilled hope as he watched the fortunes of the Children of Israel. The writer reminds us, "Delayed hope makes the heart sick, but fulfilled desire is a tree of life."[27] We are encouraged to keep on hoping, because it is the only way for our beneficiaries to have peace and a fulfilling life.

The final question is, "What hope is there for those whom we serve? There are some who learn how to avoid the snares of a dead end life. They slowly put together a vision of a better life, 'kick' certain habits, avoid destructive relationships, and often renew their faith. Some are encouraged to a more consistent regime of taking their prescribed medications, being faithful to their doctor's appointments, and discovering the path to renewed mental health.

There are other categories of challenged clients who survive, have good years and bad years, but see no future and do not seem to experience hope. Those who are extremely challenged, can also be destructive to themselves and others, and often receive harsh treatment from landlords, police, or their peers. They espouse no thought of the future or hope.

Hope in the Old Testament

The birth of hope for the Children of Israel was so memorable that generations of Jews, in spite of their situation among the nations of their world, could recite without flaw the story of their forefathers escaping slavery, coming out of the land of Egypt and being given the promise of land through their covenant with God. A way was always provided, and they journeyed from hopelessness to the hope of a great future.

Their absolute belief was that even though Moses as their leader spoke for God, it was their God who was leading them out of bondage; they were his chosen people, and God would provide a special land. "Now, therefore, if you obey my voice and keep my commandments, you shall be my treasured possession out of all peoples. Indeed, the whole earth is mine, but you shall be for me a priestly

---

27   Prv. 13:12 (CSB).

kingdom and a holy nation."[28]

Commenting on God's covenant with Israel, John Bright says, "Conditioned by this faith Israel could never take her status as a chosen people for granted; it was morally conditioned. She was no superior race, favored because she deserved it. The covenant laid heavy demands on Israel. Specifically it demanded *hesed* a grateful and complete loyalty to the God of the covenant to the exclusion of all other Gods. Equally, it demanded strict obedience to the laws of the covenant in all human relationships within the covenant relationship."[29]

Joshua, one of the first warlord leaders of the Israelites, called the 12 tribes together in the mountainous area of Shechem.[30] Their tents, cooking fires, and children flowed over the hills: the women went to and from the valley to collect water, and the men sat in circles to discuss the events of life. It was a great reunion for the tribes after the many battles that had taken place as they claimed their land. This event was a pivotal point of their changing from being a nomadic people to being an agrarian society. Joshua called them together, renewed their hope by rehearsing their history from the time of Abraham, and led them to renew their covenant to be the people of Yahweh and to worship Him alone. "With this, Israel's tribal structure assumed its classical form and Israel's history as a people may be said to have begun."[31]

At this point, "Israel was practically a classless nation, with no cleavages as we know them today. The inherent dignity of every Hebrew underlay the sense of brotherhood."[32] This common respect, which included the poor and the strangers, became one of Israel's great contributions to history. The concern for those who were impoverished, sick, challenged, imprisoned, and elderly came out of this concept that all people are kin.

---

28 Exod. 19:5-6a (NRSV).
29 John Bright, *The Kingdom of God* (Nashville: Abingdon, 1953) 29.
30 Josh. 24:1 (NIV).
31 John Bright, *A History of Israel,* Third Edition (Philadelphia: Westminster Press, 1981) 145.
32 *The Interpreter's Bible,* Vol. 2, (New York: Abingdon Press, 1953) 428.

The concept of caring for the marginalized was not new at Shechem. In Deuteronomy it is stated, "However, there shall be no poor among you, for in the land the Lord your God is giving you to possess as your inheritance, he will richly bless you, if you fully obey the Lord your God and are careful to follow all these commands I am giving you today."[33] The phrase, "there shall be no poor among you," seems to contradict the verse in the same chapter that says, "There will always be poor in the land. Therefore I command you to be openhanded toward your brothers and toward the poor and needy in your land."[34] These two verses are compatible, however, with the interpretation that if all people acted with compassion toward the poor as God was asking in verse 11, the poor would no longer be in an impoverished condition. They would have adequate means to live. Not everybody would have an equal economic situation, but everybody would be taken care of.

The care of the marginalized in their society was not noted as an appendage to the laws and commandments, but it was given as an integral part of the covenant. In the book of Leviticus, before describing the festivals, rituals, and special laws related to the year of Jubilee, it is written, "when you reap the harvest of your land, you shall not reap to the very edges of your field, or gather the fallen grapes of your vineyard; you shall leave them for the poor and the alien: I am the Lord your God... You shall not render an unjust judgment; you shall not be partial to the poor or defer to the great: with justice you shall judge your neighbor."[35] This kind of behavior would please God and was central to the life of the Israeli community.

Some social laws governing the care of the marginalized were given with a threat. "You shall not abuse any widow or orphan. If you do abuse them, when they cry out to me, I will surely heed their cry; my wrath will burn, and I will kill you with the sword, and your wives shall become widows and your children orphans."[36]

33 Deut. 15:4-5 (NIV).
34 Deut. 15:11 (NIV).
35 Lev. 19: 9-10, 15 (NIV).
36 Exod. 22:22-24 (NIV).

The covenant was powerful in three ways. First, it defined the Israelis' relationship with God. Second, it mandated how they were to treat one another and especially the poor and the strangers in their midst. There does not seem to be any reference in the Old Testament related to the care of those who were severely mentally challenged, but it seems they would come under the category of the poor. It seems their hope, or sense of a secure future, would be assumed from their village or tribe. Third, it held the loose confederation of tribes together and gave them a common hope to rally around.

During those early years there was no central government or elected officials. Leaders, strong and weak, came and went. There were times of great faithfulness and times when the covenant meant little, and kings and people worshipped other gods. But the idea of being a chosen people, destined to possess a chosen land, for a chosen purpose lived on as a promise in the mores of these tribes.

Under the kingships of David and Solomon, Jerusalem became a city known for its splendor, and the Kingdom of Israel became a dominant force in that part of the world. Because of this development, it would seem the Kingdom of Israel would be declared the Kingdom of God, but it did not happen.

Over the next centuries, the Kingdom of Israel was divided, conquered, exiled, and became a nation dispersed among nations. At times, practically the whole nation was disenfranchised from their land. In constant fear of assimilation, the hope of reestablishing their kingdom being dashed to pieces over and over, with unbelievably low morale, still there was always a remnant that remained faithful to their God, lived by the law, and held on to the concept of a future Kingdom of God. This future Kingdom of God crystallized their hope.

In the midst of the despair, Isaiah wrote, "The Spirit of the Lord God is on me, because the Lord has anointed me to bring good news to the poor. He has sent me to heal the brokenhearted, to proclaim liberty to the captives, and freedom to the prisoners."[37] This pro-

---

37   Isa. 61:1 (RSV).

phetic verse was given to a nation that had suffered at the hands of others, but it was also a reminder to those who were in difficult situations that God is near, he anoints, his deeds are to bind up the broken hearted and his message of good news brings hope.

When Jesus began his public ministry in the synagogue, he took the scroll and read Isaiah 61:1. Somehow, as Jesus pronounced those words, that same powerful hope that assures the poor and the brokenhearted that the Kingdom of God is not lost to them was experienced by those who heard.[38]

Hope in the New Testament

After Jesus was tempted in the wilderness and John had been arrested, Jesus traveled to Galilee and boldly "Preached the good news of God: The time is fulfilled, and the Kingdom of God has come near. Repent and believe in the good news."[39] One of the shocks to Jesus' audience was that the hope and dream of the Kingdom of God, which had always been talked about in the future tense, Jesus now referred to in the present tense. The paradigm shift required to understand and accept Jesus' thoughts was enormous.

Another well known verse adding to Jesus pronouncements about the Kingdom of God is found in the Lord's Prayer; "Your Kingdom come. Your will be done on earth as it is in heaven."[40] In this prayer request, there is God's Kingdom in Heaven with a representation of that same Kingdom here on earth. A basic definition of the Kingdom of God taken from this verse would be "The Kingdom of God is a society upon the earth where God's will is perfectly done as it is in heaven."[41]

Christ is at the center of this revelation. He perfectly aligned his will with that of the Father and the Kingdom of God is seen through him. One of the most revealing moments illustrating this truth was

---

38 Luke 4:18-21.
39 Mark 1:14b-15 (CSB).
40 Matt 6:10 (CSB).
41 William Barclay, *the Gospel of Matthew*, Volume 1, Revised Edition (Philadelphia: The Westminster Press, 1975) 92.

when Jesus was in the Garden of Gethsemane just before his cruci-
fixion. He prayed fervently, "My Father, if it is possible, let this cup
pass from me; yet not what I want but what you want." A few minutes later he prayed, "My Father, if this cannot pass unless I drink it,
your will be done."[42]

Participation in the Kingdom of God involves aligning one's
will with Jesus' will, which, of course, cannot be done perfectly on
one's own. Jesus promised his disciples, "But the advocate, the Holy
Spirit, whom the Father will send in my name, will teach you everything, and will remind you of all that I have said to you."[43]

As Jesus traveled from village to village and preached the
Kingdom of God, an integral part of his teaching was how those
who followed him should conduct themselves. He taught kingdom
ethics. In the Sermon on the Mount, through many of his parables,
and in the majority of his responses to peoples' questions, he provided an ethic for kingdom living.

A part of this ethic was remembering the poor, imprisoned, wid-
owed, naked, and hungry. In the parable, popularly known as "the
Parable of the Sheep and the Goats,"[44] Jesus combines a lesson on
kingdom conduct related to caring for the marginalized. The parable starts out with all of the people of the earth being sorted into
two groups. Unbeknown to those being separated, the criteria for
the separation was whether they had fed the hungry, given drink to
the thirsty, welcomed strangers, clothed the naked, or visited the
prisoners. Those who made this a part of their lifestyle were placed
in one group and allowed to claim an inheritance in "The Kingdom
of God prepared for you from the foundation of the world."[45] Those
who had not made this a part of their lifestyle had been placed in the
other group and told, "You...are accursed, depart from me into the
eternal fire prepared for the devil and his angels."[46] Jesus made this

---

42 Matt. 26:39, 42 (RSV).
43 John 14:26 (RSV).
44 Matt. 25:31-46.
45 Matt. 25:34 (NRSV).
46 Matt. 25:41 (NRSV).

scene in the parable very personal when he identified himself with the marginalized individuals who needed assistance and declared that those who were generous toward the needy had given, fed him, and cared for him. Those who were negligent of the needy had denied help to him, not just others in need.

When one studies the parables, the Sermon on the Mount, and the other teachings of Jesus, one realizes that he perfectly lived out the kingdom ethic he taught. "The unique element in Jesus teaching is that in his person the Kingdom of God has invaded human history, and men are not only placed under the ethical demand of the reign of God, but by virtue of this very experience of God's reign are also enabled to realize a new measure of righteousness."[47]

Jesus expected his followers to practice his teachings in this age and to seek righteousness in their daily lives. But as the Kingdom of God in the world is not able to fully purify or redeem this world, God's presence in believer's lives cannot fully purify or make their lives totally righteous.[48]

When Jesus taught about righteousness, he requested more than keeping the law of the Old Testament. For him, "The primary emphasis is on the inner character that underlies outward conduct."[49] If a follower is to fully keep the law, then the outward prohibitions of murder or adultery must be matched by inward prohibitions of anger and lust.

Jesus taught, "Love for one's enemies is deeper than mere kindliness in outward relationships. It involves one of the deepest mysteries of human personality and character that a man can deeply and earnestly desire that best welfare of one who would seek his hurt. This and this alone is love. It is character; it is the gift of God."[50]

The blessings of the kingdom are not a reward for righteous living because to live a perfectly righteous life in God's sight in this

---

47 George Eldon Ladd, *A Theology of the New Testament* (Grand Rapids: William B. Eerdmans, 1974) 128.
48 1 John 3:2a (NIV).
49 Ibid., 129.
50 Ibid.

world is not possible. To live out the ethics that Jesus taught should be paramount above all other considerations in a Christian's life, but the goal is not to be rewarded with a place in heaven. The purpose for following the kingdom ethics Christ taught is that the will of God will be done on earth as it is in heaven.

The blessings of the kingdom come through the redemptive work of Christ with the core issue being faith in the death, burial, and resurrection of Jesus Christ. It is through God's grace that believers participate in the work of his kingdom. This same grace brings hope into the lives of people. "God is the author and source of hope, its sustaining power, and its unseen yet certain object....hope is God-grounded, God-sustained, and God directed, hope is a reality within which men may dwell."[51]

Ministry

Christians, dedicated to the will of God, can use a secular government program to develop a faith-based Representative Payee Organization to bring a ministry of hope to challenged individuals. The staff cannot let their calling slip from the level of presenting hope to the level of only budgeting, writing checks, and paying bills.

In the beginning of this chapter, Mary, Bradley, and Lois were brought into the discussion. In spite of the many life experiences and mental challenges that separate our staff from them, what are those things that we hold in common?

First, the same as Christians cannot separate the presence of the Holy Spirit from their acts of service, we cannot separate the Holy Spirit from being an influence in the lives of those we serve. It goes back to all being created in the image of God. There is a spiritual bond between God and humanity, the eternal Spirit that permeates life as well as ministry.

Second, Jesus, in the Beatitudes says, "Blessed are the poor in

---

51   *The Interpreter's Dictionary of the Bible*, Vol. 2, s.v. "Hope."

spirit, for theirs is the kingdom of heaven."[52] This state of being "poor in spirit" should be common to all of us as Christians.

Mary, Bradley, and Lois are "poor in spirit." Because they can no longer live responsibly, I see them as living in a state of innocence like a child. Jesus said in the parable of the Sheep and Goats, "Truly I tell you, just as you did it to one of the least of these who are members of my family, you did it to me."[53]

At the same time, we are poor in spirit if we are caring for others as Christ cared for them. "Christ is lowly: he goes incognito to the poor and imprisoned. He is happiest to dwell with these least. The intensity of this oneness of Christ with mankind no words can tell. Parent and child are so closely bound that the misfortune of one becomes the equal misfortune of the other, but the bond between men and Christ is closer than any human tie. He is the Son of man has a more intimate meaning than we can grasp. There is between him and mankind a bond of the eternal Spirit…the bond between him and man is not mere nearness, but love's identity."[54]

In this identity, bridges of hope can be built and feet be set upon paths to a life well lived.

---

52 Matt. 5:3 (NRSV).
53 Matt. 25:40 (NRSV).
54 *The Interpreter's Bible,* Vol. 7 (New York: Abingdon Press, 1951) 566.

CHAPTER **8**

A FAITH-BASED AGENCY ACCEPTING FEDERAL FUNDS

Church and State

In Chicago, a fellow student asked me to tell him about our ministry at Stewards Inc. As I was steering his thoughts through the development of the ministry and how we are approved, with a letter of affirmation, from the SSA, he stopped me and asked, "I thought you were a faith based agency. How can you accept authorization to "minister" to challenged people under the Representative Payee Agency Program of the SSA? Social Security checks represent government money. Isn't this crossing the line between church and state?"

This immediately started a discussion on "What is that line?" Where and what is this legal division between church and state? Others joined in as we pooled our ignorance. We had fun doing it.

I had to go back and explain the clients' money we receive to manage is the property of the client before it comes into our system. We own the 1,600 fiduciary bank accounts that receive the client's money. Social Security says, "When the money is deposited, it is no longer the government's money."

To this my friend replied, "You still have a contract with the

SSA defining how the money is to be used and how much you can charge the clients for your services." I had to admit the question of "church and state" had crossed my mind many times, but I found it easy to justify our contract with SSA by thinking about the good we are doing.

Presently, Stewards Inc has a separate contract with Kern County Mental Health to guide the use of income for those who have very special needs. When this contract came to the Board of Directors for approval, the first question was, "Won't it compromise our witness? Can our staff and volunteers continue praying with people?" Pros and cons were discussed and the contract was accepted. The prevailing feeling was this is a new era and faith-based agencies can participate in government contracts without having to compromise their witness.

I have felt confident in our arrangements with the government, but the questions asked deserve better answers. There is a need to have a better understanding of the history and laws that govern the relationship between the church and state, and what the guidelines are that a faith-based agency should follow so as not to be compromised, yet still be able to take full advantage of funds available to support their ministry?

Church and State

First, we need to go back in history and look at the major influences that have affected the development of the relationship between the government and religious institutions in the United States.

One influence is found in our Judeo-Christian heritage. Israel of the Old Testament had both a King and a priesthood that had separate spheres of responsibility and authority. Sometimes the lines between the two were very blurred and struggles ensued, but there was a tenuous separation of the religious institution and the state.

A negative influence to this separation of church and state was inserted in history with the coming of the Roman Empire. During the centuries of this regime, the emperor was often considered to be divine and therefore to be worshipped. The government appointed the religious leaders for the empire. The Jews were exempt from worshipping the emperor and seemed to have the freedom of choosing their religious leaders and maintaining the institutions of their religion, but the Christians were not declared exempt from emperor worship and were often martyred.

The persecution of Christians ceased in CE 313 with the Edict of Milan and Christianity became the state religion of the Roman Empire in CE 380 by edict of Theodosius I. This lack of separation of church and state continued for centuries. During that time, in the West, the relationship between the Empire and the Church was always stormy and there was often an encroachment on one another's authority. In the East, Eastern Orthodoxy was the state religion and the Emperors of the Eastern Roman Empire appointed and dismissed the leaders of the church.

The shaft of light that shook the establishment and was probably the greatest influence in the development of the idea of a separate church and state came in the Protestant Reformation when Martin Luther (1483-1546) developed the idea of two kingdoms. "According to James Madison, perhaps one of the most important modern proponents of the separation of church and state, Luther's doctrine of the two kingdoms marked the beginning of the modern concept of separation of church and state."[55]

One hundred fifty years later, John Locke (1632-1704) "argued that the government lacked authority in the realm of individual conscience, as this was something rational people could not cede to the government for it or others to control…These views on religious tolerance and the importance of individual conscience, along with his social contract, became particularly influential in the American colonies and the drafting of the United States Constitution."[56]

In the First Amendment to the Constitution of the United States, ratified in 1791, the treatment of religion by the government is bro-

---

55 "Separation of church and state. Modern views." http://en.wikipedia.org.wiki.separation_of_church_and_state [accessed September 10, 2008].

56 Noah Feldman, *Divided by God* (Macmillan: Farrar, Straus and Giroux, 2005), 29.

ken into two clauses: "The establishment clause which prevents the government from establishing a national religion, providing tax money in support of religion, or otherwise favoring any single religion or religion generally; and the free exercise clause, ensuring that private religious practices are not restricted by the government."[57]

The first use of the actual phrase "separation of church and state" has been attributed to Thomas Jefferson when he wrote to the Danbury Baptists in 1802. It sums up the philosophies of that day as well as the intent of the Constitution. "Believing with you that religion is a matter which lies solely between Man & his God, that he owes account to none other for his faith or his worship, that the legitimate powers of government reach actions only, and not opinions, I contemplate with sovereign reverence that act of the whole American people which declared that their legislature should 'make no law respecting an establishment of religion, or prohibiting the free exercise thereof,' thus building a wall of separation between Church & State."[58] After this first use of the term "church and state," there is no end to its reference in letters, papers and books.

The United States was the first nation to espouse this principal. Several other nations have followed this example, but basically the United States is the leader in the world championing this complete separation of church and state.

Baptists, along with some other denominations, historically have supported the separation of church and state and, in their beginnings, suffered because of their teachings. The Catholic Church struggled with this concept until December 8, 1864 when Pope Pius IX listed the church's teaching on this subject as erroneous.

Today one is keenly aware of the struggles within the Muslim religion over this question of separation of state and religion. Most conservative Muslims would consider the separation of church and state an affront to God. But there are major liberal Muslim na-

57 "Separation of church and state. History of the Concept and Term." http://en.wikipedia. org/wiki/separation_of_church_and_state [accessed September 14, 2008].
58 "Separation of Church and State. Modern Views." http://en.wikipedia.org/wiki/separation_of_church_and_state [accessed September 10, 2008].

tions such as Turkey, Senegal, Bosnia, Indonesia, Herzegovina and Azerbaijan that maintain secular governments. Every one of these governments struggles to survive.

The quality of the separation between church and state needs to be kept in mind. In the United States, citizens are so accustomed to a friendly relationship, rather than one of hostility, that the idea is taken for granted. One only needs to look around the world or into history to see how blessed we are for this quality of a relationship. A recent example of hostility is when the church in Romania demonstrated against the dictator Caeseceau and forced the downfall of his government. The French, Mexican, and Spanish Revolutions are other famous examples of hostility and war between the church and state.

There is no doubt that the reason for America's peaceful existence can be traced back to the founders of the nation. The planners of the United States government and constitution did not make the separation of church and state a separate issue but an issue among many others that needs to be guarded and guided by the full democratic processes. It is this holistic approach that continues to help maintain a friendly relationship between the church and state in the United States.

Faith Organizations Caring for the Marginalized

Up to this point, the summary of history in this chapter has covered government programs designed to help retirees and those who are challenged to live out their years with adequate food, shelter, and clothing. At the same time along side these government programs, across the United States, there have been thousands of faith-based organizations and churches with a myriad of programs that have been an expression of compassion for those marginalized in society. George Bush, the 41st president, called these programs "a thousand points of light." Until recently, because of legal restrictions on the expression of their faith, most faith-based organizations did not accept funds from the United States Government. Those accepting contracts and funding from any level of government were willing to accept the possibility of having the expression of their faith restricted.

During the era, when a faith-based organization was required to restrict its testimony, there was a point at which the government and faith-based organizations converged. It was Section 501(c)3 of the Internal Revenue Code. This made it possible for non-profit organizations, to make a charitable contribution to their community through their programs and be exempt from taxes and for those who donated to this service to be free from taxation on their contributions.

All faith-based organizations have accepted the 501(c)3 status, but most of them refused government support for programs because they did not want their ability to express their faith compromised.

The Rescue Mission movement has been a large well-known faith-based ministry that falls in this category. The Association of Gospel Rescue Missions has 315 missions across the United States. Throughout the years these missions would not compromise their witness and depended on private contributions to continue their programs. The first Rescue Mission in the United States set the standard for the decades ahead. "The New York City Rescue Mission was started by the now infamous Jerry McAuley in the 1860s. In short, he was a former alcoholic who was radically converted while in Sing Sing prison."[59] Over the years, untold millions of dollars have been raised for the Rescue Missions' well known ministries, but none from the government. It has all been by private donations as this faith-based organization has spread across the U.S.

In the last couple of years, with the new laws governing the relationship between faith-based organizations and the State, a few of the Rescue Missions have started contracting with the United States government to fund certain programs. In Bakersfield, the Rescue Mission contracts with all levels of government for support for certain programs, yet maintains a strong program of Bible study and witnessing.

59 *History of the Association of Gospel rescue Missions.* http://www.agrm.org/history. html [accessed October 29, 2008].

Some faith-based ministries, like Catholic Charities, however have found ways to distance their expression of faith in some programs and have been accepting government support for decades. "Catholic Charities, the largest private network of social service organizations in the United States works to support families, reduce poverty, and build communities."[60] Seventeen hundred charities, with a combined budget of over one billion dollars, make up this organization. Many of these charities are separately incorporated and can accept government funding even though they are required to look to the diocesan bishop for guidance.

The Salvation Army's mission statement is "The ultimate mission of the Salvation Army is to bring the whole world under the Christian umbrella."[61] Early in the life of the Salvation Army in the United States, moving into disaster areas quickly became part of their program. The first great disaster in which they joined the relief effort was the hurricane devastation of Galveston, Texas, in 1900. Out of this experience, they realized they needed to accept government money to have adequate relief to take to emergency situations. The government justified funding the Salvation Army by pointing out the nature of the relief they could provide.

Another faith-based organization that has accepted government funds for decades is the Lutheran Social Services (LSS) of Wisconsin and Upper Michigan. "Until the 1960's, the organization primarily provided child welfare services and programs for single mothers. Then, about 40 years ago, LSS contracted with state and local governments to help people in need. This partnership initiated a rapid expansion of offerings to the community."[62] Today this faith-based ministry has a yearly budget of $76,000,000 of which $51,000,000 is funded by various levels of government.

In summary, for two centuries there has been a legal and theo-

---

60 "Catholic Charities, USA – Providing Help. Creating Hope." http://www.catholiccharitiesusa.org [accessed October 29, 2008].

61 "The Salvation Army." http://en.wikipedia.org/wiki/Salvation_Army#United_States [accessed October 30, 2008].

62 "History of Lutheran Social Services." http://www.lsswis.org/AboutUs/history.htm [accessed October 30, 2008].

logical division between government funded programs and privately
supported faith-based ministry programs. But, in the last 50 years,
with the growing marginalized population in the United States, the
barriers between government funding and faith-based initiatives
have been coming down. This change developed without a change
in the Constitution or the laws governing economic relations between the church and state. "In a 1982 study by F. Ellen Netting
focusing on government funding of Protestant social service agencies in one Midwestern city, he found that some agencies received
between 60 and 80 percent of their support from the government
and that approximately half of their combined budgets were government financed. In 1994 government funding accounted for 65
percent of the nearly two billion dollar annual budget of Catholic
Charities USA, and 75 percent of the revenues of the Jewish Board
of Family and Children's Services."[63] There have been problems
and questions over the years since each of these ministries is un-
questionably sectarian. But the problems have been solved through
unspoken understandings or just plain not talking about it. The few
complaints registered during this time had to do "with required religious activities, especially with required attendance at Sunday
church services."[64]

Charitable Choice

By 1996, Congress was conscious of the change that was taking
place in the relationship between the church and state in regard to
the funding of social services. In that year, at President Clinton's
urging, "as a part of comprehensive welfare reform legislation,
Congress enacted Section 104 of the Personal Responsibility and
Work Opportunity Reconciliation Act of 1996 (PWORA). That provision, which has come to be known as "Charitable Choice," has
subsequently been included in Welfare-to-Work legislation, the
Community Services Block Grant Program, the Substance Abuse

63   Sheila Suess Kennedy, *Privatization and Prayer: The Challenge of Charitable Choice,*
     A manuscript filed at the University of Indiana. 2.
64   Ibid., 2.

and Mental Health Services Administration's drug treatment programs, and the Children's Health Act. Charitable Choice has been heralded as a new and promising approach to delivery of government social services through state contracts with "faith-based organizations," or FBOs."[65]

Charitable Choice is designed to open the door for faith-based organizations to use certain federal funds in their charitable community work. The guiding principles in this legislation are:

1. A level playing field. Faith-based providers are eligible to compete for funds on the same basis as any other providers, neither excluded nor included because they are religious, too religious or of the wrong religion.

2. Respect for allies. The religious character of faith-based providers is protected by allowing them to retain control over the definition, development, practice, and expression of their religious beliefs. Neither federal nor state governments can require a religious provider to alter its form of internal governance or remove religious art, icons, scripture or other symbols in order to be a program participant.

3. Protecting clients. In regard to rendering assistance, religious organizations shall not discriminate against an individual on the basis of religion, a religious belief, or refusal to actively participate in a religious practice. If an individual objects to the religious character of a program, a secular alternative must be provided.

4. Church-State separation. All government funds must be used to fulfill the public social service goals, and no direct government funding can be diverted to inherently religious activities such as worship, sectarian instruction, and proselytization.[66]

A person can quickly assume that before this enactment by the Congress there would be widespread debate and controversy in the

---

65 Ibid., 2.
66 "What is Charitable Choice." http://www.hhs.gov/fbci/choice.html [accessed February 16, 2009].

chambers. To the contrary, what little Senate debate there was on Charitable Choice focused on the provision's constitutionality. The proponents of Charitable Choice continue to point out that FBOs have an enormous reserve of people with know-how and a will to develop social services. These FBOs may be unwilling to secularize or mute their testimony, but they are more motivated in their call to this type of service and therefore are more effective than government or secular agencies. Based on my experience, we should add that FBOs are less expensive to support compared to secular and government organizations.

The opponents to Charitable Choice have some question about the effectiveness of FBOs, but their main objection is that this measure erodes the constitutional separation of church and state. At first, Charitable Choice left those who are the public administrators of this new approach with little direction and with thorny questions, such as, "how to identify and recruit the 'faith Based organizations' targeted by these initiatives, how to evaluate and augment their capacity to deliver services, and how to encourage their increased participation while adhering to constitutional principles."[67]

Some of the public administrators are Christians and have an understanding of the theological differences among the various denominations. Others do not have this experience, which leads to misunderstandings. One of the major misunderstandings is a theological issue within the conservative segment of the religious community. There can be a fundamental belief that the root cause of individuals being marginalized in society is their lack of faith in Jesus Christ. They would argue the only way for those who live in poverty to become contributing members of society is that they become transformed through faith in Christ. Therefore, a part of their program must include requiring attendance at worship services and proselytizing.

However, most faith-based organizations that carry out their ministry in the name of Christ are gratified when a person becomes

---

67 Ibid., 2.

a believer but do not feel it is the sole reason for ministry to others. They also see the presence of those who live in poverty as a societal issue requiring programs such as job training, school reform, food subsidy programs and counseling. With this approach to solving the problems of the poor and jobless as the design of a faith-based or-ganization's program, the opposition disappears and is replaced by affirmation.

Recent Developments

In 1998, Mark Chavez made a study using data collected by the National Congregation Study "to determine the extent to which congregations might be inclined to take advantage of the funding opportunities offered by Charitable Choice."[68] He found that con-gregations of 900 or more members tended to look favorably on the new opportunities and accepted public funding for their social pro-grams. Smaller congregations did not get involved as much because it was too difficult to start social service programs that could attract federal funds. His study showed that black congregations were five times more likely to participate in programs that utilize government funding. Also, liberal congregations were more likely to develop programs and request support through government funds than con-servative churches.

In the ensuing years, few churches have directly applied to use government programs. It seems to me that parachurch organizations are the entities that have developed a greater willingness to accept these funds. Part of this willingness comes out of the scarcity of funds available to them outside of government funding. When they look at available funding, from all levels of government, they dis-cover a large reservoir.

President George W. Bush took the Charitable Choice Provision one step further by establishing the White House Office of Faith-based and Community Initiatives (OFBCI) on January 29, 2001. Understanding that "Faith-based and community organizations

---

68   Ibid., 4.

(FBCOs) have a long tradition of helping Americans in need and together represent an integral part of our nations social service network"[69] This initiative seeks to put FBCOs on an equal footing with other organizations in competing for funds. John Dilulio, Jr., the first director of the office made known that he wanted FBCOs to compete on the same basis as other non-governmental providers of these services, and do so without having to hide their religious basis.

For fiscal year 2005, more than $2.2 billion in competitive social service grants were awarded to faith-based organizations. The assumption is that prior to the passage of Charitable Choice, faith-based organizations could contract with the government only if they were willing to secularize by at least masking their roots and identities. This initiative, the development of the OFBCI, was to level the playing field. Whether Christian, Jewish, Muslim, Hindu or another religion, one's identity did not have to be hidden, and each similar program would have equal access to winning contracts and appropriations.

Opponents to this initiative raise the possibility of bias when all FBCOs declare their faith. They say the use of faith-based terminology is a subtext of the larger culture war, and the issue is not whether religious organizations should be receiving government funding but rather which contractors should be preferred. The question comes down to those making the decisions as to whom to grant funds. Would they grant the funds on the basis of their own religious preference or would they grant the funds on the basis of ability to carry out their program?

A point in favor of having the FBCOs declare their faith is that those awarding contracts or funds to support their programs would

---

69 "White House Faith-Based & Community Initiative. The Initiative in Action." http://www.whitehouse.gov/government/fbci/president-initiative.html [accessed September 18, 2008]. All of the White House sites, related to this subject and established under President Bush, have been suspended since January 21, 2009. The material in this section is a summary of that which was printed and now suspended. Under the administration of President Obama, these sites have been renewed in a different format and wording. It will take some study to see if the content has changed.

know if there is a faith contradiction between what they are proposing and that which their faith will allow them to provide. The example that is used over and over is the prohibition of birth control by the Catholic Church. If they received funding for their family planning centers, would they prohibit the distribution of condoms and the training needed for birth control if that is a part of the government requirement? This point requires some sophistication of the public administrators to know the practical theology of the FBCOs.

Proponents of Charitable Choice and the OFBCI give the following general reasons for supporting the new initiatives. First, FBCOs appear to emphasize thrift and individual responsibility in the way they carry out their services and in their expectations of those they serve. Second, these agencies require less government to carry out the agreed upon services. They raise other support and use more volunteers. Third, they are more responsive and flexible when change is necessary to accomplish goals or when new needs arise. Fourth, they are closer to their clients and allow them to join in their rehabilitation or meeting their own needs. Fifth, this initiative makes it possible for those "thousand points of light" to receive support. There are thousands of smaller very capable agencies that could reach out further in their service to their community if they had additional support.

The OFBCI projects three other major concerns. First, the initiative is concerned with extending Charitable Choice provisions so that possible discrimination against FBCOs cannot happen. Second, this initiative is concerned with the protection of the religious freedom of the beneficiaries. Benefits cannot be used or withheld to force anyone to join the faith of the provider. Third, this initiative is to protect the hiring rights of the faith-based charities. A public administrator cannot interfere with the hiring rights that legally are assigned to the FBCOs.

Since President Obama's inauguration, the United States Department of Health and Human Services posted on-line a directive to state and local officials on *Partnering with Faith-Based and*

Community Organizations.[70] This 10 page directive gives a history of the changes that have taken place over the last two decades, while stating again the initiatives and regulations that govern the use of public funding by faith-based organizations that have programs dedicated to charitable purposes.

One of the major questions is whether accepting public funds will require the hiring of employees that do not have the same faith values. This directive affirms that, "There is no general federal law that prohibits FBOs that receive federal funds from hiring on a religious basis. Nor does Title VII of the Civil Rights Act of 1964, which applies regardless of whether an organization receives federal funds, prohibit FBOs from hiring on a religious basis...It should be noted, however, that while in general an FBO retains this religious hiring autonomy even if it receives federal assistance, certain laws and regulations may place independent conditions on the receipt of specific government funds."[71] These laws and regulations deal with the treatment of benefactors by the FBO.

For instance, there will be no discrimination based on religion, race, or gender; benefactors will not be required to attend worship experiences; and proselytizing will not be a part of the services being rendered.

Conclusion

Every time I read about the study and work the framers of the United States Constitution and the early architects of our government put into developing our nation, I am inspired anew. What an accomplishment! I feel as if I am following along on hallowed ground as I read about the discussion and arguments that have taken place over a whole history of world experience and ideas. Finally, Americans enjoy, and are charged to maintain what they created. It makes me very conservative when it comes to accepting any small change in the interpretation of that to which they agreed. They were

70 "Partnering with Faith-Based and Community Organizations." http://www.whitehouse.gov/government/fbci/guidance/partnering.html [accessed February 15, 2009].
71 Ibid., 9.

great wordsmiths and packed rich meaning into each sentence. They looked so deeply into the life of a new nation, and understood those principals that would not only endure but would serve to guide our fledgling nation into maturity.

When it comes to reinterpreting a sentence or two that provides guidance for the idea of the separation of the church and state, I don't feel our national leaders are on a slippery slope, but I feel citizens must keep all branches of our government strong and democratic in order to guide this reinterpretation. To honor the constitution, the church should never take over the government. At the same time the government should never take over the church. I feel that neither of these will happen under the present laws if the church accepts government funds and contracts in order to aid church ministries that help the needy in our communities. It seems that both the church and the government have their checks and balances in place to be able to work in partnership with one another to ameliorate life in communities.

There is one caution I think needs to be pointed out. Agencies gravitating toward those places in the economy where they can find more adequate support, at the same time often evolve from being a faith-based agency to being just another secular non-profit agency. This caution does not imply the leaders are not Christians, but their approach to the service they are giving the community loses its Christian distinctive.

One restriction that keeps coming up in the government guidelines for use of public money is that these funds cannot be used for proselytizing. "Proselytism is the practice of attempting to convert people to another opinion and, particularly, another religion."[72]

Jesus espoused proselytizing. The classic verse is Mark 8:34 when Jesus addressed the crowd and said, "If anyone would come after me, he must deny himself and take up his cross and follow me."[73] This had nothing to do with food, shelter, clothing, healing,

---

72 "Proselytism." http://www.answers.com/topic/proselytism [accessed March 13, 2009].

73 Mark 8:34 (NIV).

or a stipend. In fact, if Christians take up the cross and truly follow Jesus they might, instead, give up a United States standard of food, shelter, or clothing.

On the other hand, when Jesus gave food, forgiveness, and healing, there were no conditions such as "take up your cross and follow me" required. Sometimes there were hopes and offers of a more abundant life, but no conditions.

I became very conscious of this approach when I lived and worked in the city of Kinshasa, the capital of the Democratic Republic of Congo. In those turbulent days of anarchy, there were hundreds of thousands of children who needed an education. The Muslims came in with their petrol dollars and offered an education to all who would become a Muslim. Our Christian friends had a struggle over that offer. I thought this is the way of other religions, but not Christianity. Then there was the day I met a fundamental group of Christian missionaries who were withholding medical help and education until the needy person became a Christian.

I believe strongly in witnessing, but only after I have won the right to witness, and the person to whom I am witnessing is not at the disadvantage of need. Appropriate proselytizing should be determined by the choice of adhering to Christ's example and should not need to be guided by government rules.

After reading the rules governing expressions of faith while using government funds, I cannot see any reason why an FBCO should not use government funds and contracts to meet the needs of people in their community.

If the sole purpose of a ministry is to bring individuals to Christ, then government funds should not be a part of the ministry's support. If, within that ministry, there are other goals that target needs in the community, then I think Christians can partner with the government in confidence that they are within the law and without pressure to compromise their ministry.

CHAPTER 9

SUMMARY

The Ministry of Hope

She was well dressed and her demeanor was professional. Perhaps that is why we were surprised when the rather flabbergasting remarks came out of her mouth. "You mean to tell me that you would take folks who are on drugs and alcohol as clients? You would manage the SSI income for people who are certifiably mentally ill, bi-polar and schizophrenic patients? The homeless and disruptive group could come into your offices and you would manage some of their eccentricities as well as income and help them find housing?"

After each question we nodded our heads while murmuring, "Yes, that's our ministry and commitment to service as we partner with Social Security." We were getting fired up as a team and more committed to the purpose of our visit as she began to wind down with an admission of, "I didn't know there was an organization that would do that for us. As an employee of Social Security, I often just have to terminate the benefits of people who are misusing their income; I have no one to help them and they are disruptive to our processes."

This event that some staff members and I experienced recently, crystallizes both the struggle and purpose for this proposal of a ministry using government channels as a redemptive force in the ever-growing population that struggles with the manifold challenges that often prohibit the abundant life that Jesus promises in his New Testament conversations.

The hope that one dreams of igniting in this ministry inspires roads to the future. Moving from rejection to the possibility of a redeemed and fruitful life is the journey that one hopes to facilitate despite the barriers and challenges that confront the marginalized. In a lecture given by Dr. Wayne Gordon, he said, "Hopelessness is the greatest problem in our marginalized communities."[74]

Some of those needing help in the management of their incomes are not caught in the spiral of use. Instead, they are trying to lead clean and sober lives and face other challenges such as reasoning ability, background, trauma, knowledge and education, family drama, lack of motivation and encouragement, involvement in a family system of public dependence, physical or mental disabilities, and mood disorders. The list goes on but terminates at making the individual unemployable in most instances. Often, challenged individuals are compelled to seek help from an agency because their income has been suspended until they sign up with an approved RPO. Frequently they come into the program with mixed emotions of distrust, fear, anger, and despair. They come to regain their income stream, but we strive to offer much more in suggested patterns of discipline, savings, payment of bills when due, payment of rent, and caretaking of both the physical and relational aspects of their lives.

We strive to offer patience, for that is often in short supply in difficult relationships. One tends to give up too quickly and write off people who annoy us. The love Paul writes about in the book of Romans is based on God's patience with us. He considered patience an active energy that merges into hope.[75] In an electronic era with instant communication, people expect quick and easy fixes to complex problems and are frustrated with incremental progress.

---

74 Dr. Wayne Gordon, known as "Coach," founded the Lawndale Community Church on Chicago's West side, in the fifteenth poorest neighborhood in the United States.

75 Rom. 5:4.

"Profound change, however, is ordinarily a step-by-step process that takes time. Our patience grows from the conviction that God is at work in our lives."[76]

The ministry of a local RPO is not the only or perfect solution to the myriad of ills that face the complex lives of the marginalized segment of society. However, the theological and Biblical underpinnings that illuminate the concept of hope in this environment make them viable roads to wholeness.

Patiently dealing with the problems and perspectives of the lives of beneficiaries is not for the fainthearted or easily discouraged. The patience born of love is basic to the sharing of trust in a relationship, and the discipline that does not scold and judge, but seeks the best for another person is what wins the right to guide another. Advice given is not advice received until the recipient is open to listening and living in new territory.

Like all good ministry programs, the RPO needs to work in alliance with other agencies that care about the same marginalized people. These agencies include the Rescue Mission, Homeless Center, Alliance Against Family Violence, Food Bank, Gleaners, AA, NA, NAMI, and other support groups and churches sensitive to challenged people.

God's purposes for his creation and his best plan for each of our lives are revealed through the encouragement of the redemptive community. It is only through deeply desiring the best for others that we discover the high adventures that are planned for our own journeys.

---

76 "Patient Living." *Christianity Today Online.* www.christianitytoday.com/workplace/articles/character/patientliving.html [accessed January 19, 2009].

PART 2
A Guide for Developing a Representative Payee Organization

This guide is dedicated to the 1,000's of beneficiaries
who have streamed through the doors
of Stewards Inc over the years.

While this writing is about reframing a

government program into a Christian ministry,

it really is not about process.

It is not as much about working with Social Security

or budgeting income for those receiving Social Security

as it is about people who need hope for the future.

This guide is concerned with the God given vision and purpose

of being instrumental in bringing hope and light into the lives of others.

Truly experiencing life means having the security of knowing

that one has a future.

For some who have lost their way,

the futility and challenges of daily life brings desperation.

Hope is defined by the reality that life springs from God's creative,

sustaining power and moves toward good which is congruent with

God's purpose and promise.

The living and sharing of that truth may take many different forms

but it is a high call and worthy adventure.

Gloria P. Marshall

GUIDE TO DEVELOPING A FAITH-BASED REPRESENTATIVE PAYEE ORGANIZATION

Introduction

The purpose of this chapter is to be a companion piece to the Social Security Administration (SSA) publication, *Representative Payment Program, Guide for Organizational Representative Payees, 2008*[77]. The SSA publication, written from the SSA perspective, is like a wall socket ready to deliver electricity into a room. This chapter makes the SSA publication useful like the plug, cord, and lamp that utilizes the power in the socket to bring light to a space. Together the SSA guide and this chapter can facilitate the development of a faith-based Representative Payee Organization (RPO).

For the development of Stewards Inc, a faith-based RPO, I led our team through all of the steps explained in this chapter to produce the organization we have today. We had no idea what the journey would require from start to finish, but took each step as we discovered what was needed to continue. The journey has required work and financial sacrifice but as the organization has grown, the blessings have brought joy and fulfillment as a balance.

In the beginning, it is good to lightly read both pieces through for an overview of the project. The steps for developing a RPO, as a non-profit corporation and a ministry, are presented, section by section, in the sequence required to be successful. Complete one step at a time. Rushing to the next step before the last step is completed will cause delay.

---

77   This manual is produced by the Social Security Administration, Office of Beneficiary and Determination Services, SSA Publication No. 17-013, ICN 443170. The online address for this publication is, http://www.socialsecurity.gov/about.htm   For quicker service telephone (410) 965-2039.

Development of a Board of Directors

Each step of the way, as your organization grows, funding sources, other agencies, and government offices will ask, "Who is your Board of Directors?" Sometimes this means, "Do you have a Board of Directors?" But often it means, "Tell me about the individuals who make up your Board!"

It is possible an existing Board for another program might want to add the RPO program to their ministry if the two programs are compatible. This works well when the established Board already has a good reputation in the community.

If this is not the case and the RPO is new to the community, the person with the vision needs to start by choosing persons of faith who share the vision to form a Board of Directors. Diversity in gender and ethnicity should be a part of this process.

There are four reasons the leader needs to carefully choose the right people to form the initial Board for the development of the faith-based RPO. First, the Board can serve as prayer partners. Prayer brings a spiritual unity and spiritual support to the project that cannot be created in any other way.

Second, the Board of Directors can become a loving watchdog for those events that can make it difficult for the project to advance and be a resource to search out solutions to problems that crop up. The Executive Director or Manager administrates the daily activities of the organization as the Board sets the policies that will guide the program into the future.

Third, the Board becomes the organization's face in the community, before the ministry has developed its own persona. Their faith in the ministry being developed will be contagious and opens doors for all kinds of needed support. Social Security, Banks and other institutions respond more readily to people they know and trust than to programs just being developed.

Fourth, a Board of Directors is needed to develop the Articles of Incorporation and By-laws for the organization. Do not rush out and hire a lawyer. Read the section of this chapter entitled *Developing a Non-profit Corporation, 501(c)3.*

Often the question is raised as to whether someone on staff can be a member of the Board of Directors. Legally, up to 49 percent of the Board can be on staff, can have a relative of blood lineage or an in-law on staff, or provide a loan to the agency. At Stewards Inc we have a policy to keep our limit at 33 percent. Some funding groups require a complete separation of the staff and the Board of Directors.

When the Board of Directors is small, it can easily be enlarged as needed. The existing Board can vote to change the number of people on the Board, and this change needs to be clearly noted in the minutes. After the Articles of Incorporation and By-laws are filed with the State, the number of Board members can still be changed. The new number needs to be typed into the By-laws, but the State does not need to be notified of this change. The State is more interested in any changes in the Articles of Incorporation than in the By-laws.

The designated number of members for the Board of Directors should be an odd number. This is not a legal requirement, but a practical point. It saves the possibility of having a tie vote.

In order not to create a self-perpetuating Board, when the Board of Directors first meets, it should decide the length of each person's term so that re-election is staggered over the years and there is a set length of service. Most Board members are elected for three years and can serve for two full terms. Those members starting with a one or two year term can be re-elected to serve two full terms.

There are many good resources outlining the duties of Board members but there are two cardinal rules that should be understood and taught that help maintain harmony on the Board and between the Staff and Board. First, the Board of Directors develops all policy and the Administrator of the staff and program makes all administrative decisions. The Chairperson of the Board must make sure that all business coming before the Board is related to policy and the Administrator must make sure all administrative decisions are in harmony with the set policies. Second, the Chairperson of the Board cannot make unilateral decisions for the Board. The Chairperson's duty is to convene the Board and lead the Board as reports, programs, concerns, and questions are discussed and voted on.

The Board speaks with one voice and individual Board members have power only when sitting in a group and in agreement.

Stewards Inc was started by three families, one of which was ours. One person in each family became a Board member. Gloria, my wife, who has been extremely involved in developing Stewards Inc, was the Board member from our family. At the same time, in the beginning years, she was the administrator helping develop staff and office systems that became necessary as the organization grew. I was the Executive Director working with clients, guiding the banking, and being our representative to Social Security.

Now, Stewards Inc has 11 board members who vote and three emeritus members who do not vote.

The Board of Directors can meet before the Articles of Incorporation and the By-laws are filed with the State. A Chairperson and Secretary should be chosen and minutes kept of all proceedings. Minutes of discussions do not have to be kept, but all votes and decisions must be recorded.

The question is sometimes asked, "When a person is interviewed as a candidate for membership on the Board of a faith-based organization, can they be asked about their faith?" The answer is "Yes." When an agency declares it is a faith-based agency, it does not have to accept anyone who will compromise that faith. Even if the faith-based organization is receiving government funds for services they have contracted to provide to the larger community, they do not have to limit the asking of that question. However, if the Board shuts out the larger community and is not diversified in ethnicity, gender, and expressions of Christian faith, it will limit its contact and response from the community. Some foundations now ask for the ethnicity and gender breakdown of the Board of

Directors. It comes full circle to the question asked at the beginning of this section, "Who is your Board of Directors?"

Developing a Non-Profit Corporation, 501(c)3

As a 501(c)3 corporation is being formed, every level of government has requirements. For every level, forms must be completed and evidences submitted. Globally, it looks daunting, but submitting the forms and documents step by step is not difficult. Every level of government is on-line with forms and guidance. Templates are available for the papers that need to be initiated on-line and in publications. The various levels of government encourage individuals who are a part of the developing enterprise to do this paperwork on their own. Besides saving money, a great advantage is the person administrating the forms and presentations will understand the business in a way that will help in the future.

There are two sources of help that are invaluable. First are the government on-line sites. They are very user friendly. Second is a book called *How to Form a Nonprofit Corp.*[78] These two sources of help compliment one another and make it unnecessary to hire someone else to do the work required to form the corporation.

The following administrative steps are in the sequence they need to be completed:

1. The first matter of business for the Board is to select a name for the non-profit corporation and establish a statement of purpose. The name does not necessarily have to be descriptive of the program.

In selecting a name for the non-profit corporation, it is required that the name is not being used by another corporation in the state. Every state has a similar internet site for checking a name to determine if it is already being used. If it is not being used, one can put a hold on it. In California, the internet address is www.sos.ca.gov/business/ California Secretary of State – Business Portal. Corporations. Name Availability. The instructions are easy to follow in order to

---

78   Anthony Mancuso, *How to Form a Nonprofit Corporation* (Berkeley: Nolo Press, 2005). http://www.nolo.com

secure a name. While researching, have several agreed upon names in mind.

2. Writing the statement of purpose should be undertaken by those dedicated to the ministry. In one or two sentences describe the purpose of your ministry. This statement of purpose will not only be written into your Articles of Incorporation, but will be presented over and over in reports and requests for funding.

The statement of purpose presently found in our Articles of Incorporation is "Stewards Inc exists to ignite hope and inspire futures of those who need assistance budgeting their disability and retirement incomes by being a Representative Payee Organization that recognizes the worth and dignity of each person by providing financial counsel, good stewardship and guidance toward an abundant life for each beneficiary." This is a very narrow statement that applies to just one kind of program. If a Board's goal is to couple the Representative Payee program with other programs a much broader statement should be used.

3. The next matter of business for the Board is to write the Articles of Incorporation and the By-laws. This is a simple formality, if your Board of Directors is established, the name for your organization has been selected, and the statement of purpose is agreed upon. The Articles of Incorporation declare your organization is a "Public Benefit Corporation," the name and purpose of your non-profit corporation, the business address, and names the members of the original Board.

The By-laws describe the business structure of the Board and the responsibilities of the officers and members of the Board. A major statement in the By-laws is that the Board members cannot be held liable for any suits brought against the corporation.

Because the major decisions are made before the Articles of Incorporation and the By-laws are written, the actual writing is a simple process. The CD in the Nolo Press book has all of the forms necessary and it takes about two hours to fill in the blanks. The book guides the person filling out the forms about where to send them and the fees that are required. The total fees are about $350 (2009).

The legal departments of Social Security, Kern County, and three banks have scrutinized our papers without raising a question.

The State will respond with a letter affirming that you are indeed a 501(c)3 non-profit corporation of your state.

4. The next step is applying for federal 501(c)3 tax exemption. The easiest way to complete IRS Form 1023, Application for Recognition of Exemption, is to follow the instructions in the Nolo Press book. The information is routine and a bit tedious to record except for one point. Your corporation, a public benefit corporation, must request "public charity status" for the kind of service to the community the corporation is offering. The rationale is that this corporation will be a publicly supported corporation through multiple donations. Churches and schools receive this designation automatically, but this kind of a public benefit corporation could carelessly be classified as a foundation and the rules governing foundations are different.

When you receive the letter of exemption, make copies and carefully file the original.

5. A Federal Tax Identification Number or Employer Identification Number is to be requested after the letter of tax exemption is received. The best way to request the E.I.N. is on-line. The way to find the right place on-line is to Google: E.I.N. Go to Employer ID Numbers. Go to: How to Apply for an E.I.N.

The E.I.N. becomes a major source of identity to be used on all federal and state reports as well as all papers submitted to Social Security to conduct daily business.

6. At the state level, obtaining the state tax exemption is dependent on obtaining the federal tax exemption. A copy of the federal tax exemption can be used in a letter to the state. Again, it is easy to follow the Nolo Press book in presenting this request to the Franchise Board of the state.

7. Most counties require that before a non-profit corporation commences their business in the county they must declare the name

under which they will conduct their activities. This is called a d.b.a. "doing business as" requirement. It may be the name of your non-profit corporation, but if you have a different name for your program then it needs to be the program name. The easiest way to register your "d.b.a." is to telephone the county department of licenses and ask for their online procedures. There will be a requirement that you advertise this name in the community and the license department will advise on how to do this.

8. Cities have a licensing requirement for businesses that are for profit. Most cities do not require non-profit corporations to have a license.

9. The wrap up for this part of the development is called the "First Meeting of the Board of Directors." The results of the development of the corporation must be written into the minutes. All of the papers that have been filed and all of the responses that have been received from all levels of government must be noted in the minutes. The officers of the Board should be named in the minutes. The selection of the bank for the corporation's accounts is finalized by a vote of the Directors. All of the procedures for that First Meeting are described in the Nolo Press book.

This does not mean it is the first time the Board of Directors has met. It does mean that the corporation has turned a corner and is ready for business.

One of the most important forms a non-profit public benefit corporation must file yearly is the IRS Form 990. The IRS instructions suggest that an organization wait until it is receiving $25,000 in yearly receipts before filing this form. This sum is not the total of the income of those beneficiaries being served, but it is the total of the income received to support the business side of the organization. In spite of the IRS directions, do not wait until the income reaches $25,000. Within a year your organization will be at that level and it is good to have started the process.

Fill form 990 out carefully. IRS posts the completed form on the internet and it becomes public knowledge. Foundations to which you might apply for a grant or other agencies with whom you want to collaborate will look up your Form 990 on-line and know all about your organization, finances, Board members and the extent of your programs.

Part VI, Sections A, B, and C, of Form 990 is a compliance section asking if your organization is complying with different federal regulations. Never answer "no." Always determine what needs to honestly happen so that you can answer "yes." These regulations are good guidelines that will strengthen the business and compliance side of your non-profit corporation.

Agency Location

There are six major considerations regarding the location of a RPO's office. The first is transportation. The office should be located near a hub for public transportation. The ideal is having each beneficiary show up at the office once a month so their situation and condition can be evaluated face to face. The task of a payee is more than doling out checks for beneficiaries, but is really about caring for them in their life situations. They may only come to your office for a few minutes to pick up their weekly food check, but that contact is important. If transportation is too difficult, beneficiaries will request their check be sent in the mail, and personal contact becomes limited. Of course, some beneficiaries may be house bound and routine administration has to be over the telephone and checks sent through the mail.

The second major consideration is the close proximity of a branch of the bank that holds the accounts. Beneficiaries need to be able to cash their checks without a charge and the bank that keeps their fiduciary accounts is the only place that will give them this service. Eventually stores will come to respect the checks written by your ministry organization but this does not happen until the RPO's reputation is established. At the same time, there is a lot of paper work that needs to be carried between the RPO's office and the customer service representative of the bank. As the number of clients grows, this can become a daily trip since the bank wants papers with original signatures.

The third is the nature of the stores in the area that surrounds the new office. If the businesses do not cater to the needs of marginalized individuals, they will informally unite in their resentment of people traffic that does not benefit them, and make it very difficult to continue your service to the community. These merchants will register complaints to the Downtown Business Association, Better Business Association, and the Police Department. They do not want the beneficiaries lounging around their businesses. On the other hand, if the adjoining businesses cater to marginalized individuals, they will be very helpful. Small markets encourage the presence of an RPO. With their higher prices and small sales, they can turn a profit. Unfortunately, many of the user friendly businesses also sell alcoholic beverages. Even if the beneficiary's check has a memo that says 'no alcoholic beverages,' it is difficult to ensure the merchant will honor it.

A fourth consideration is public restrooms. If there are none in the area of the RPO and the RPO does not provide restrooms, the beneficiaries will urinate and defecate in surrounding storefront entries, parking lots, and allies. The community reaction to this is understandably negative. Restrooms must be provided. Stewards Inc. finally provided restrooms at a considerable cost and 99.9 percent of the beneficiaries respect them and keep them clean.

A fifth consideration is parking. It is surprising how many beneficiaries have a friend giving them transportation. On the first and third of the month, as well as every Monday, parking will be a problem if there is not a designated area of at least 15 or 20 spaces that can be used exclusively by the beneficiaries without bothering the neighbors.

The sixth is the area of the city where many of the potential beneficiaries live. Locating in this area and relating to the Social Security office that serves this area will enhance the potential number of referrals that will come from Social Security.

Building a Relationship with the SSA

A RPO must develop a relationship with the Social Security office that services the zip code area where the new RPO's office will be located. The relationship developed must be respectful and amicable because there will be daily interaction as the new organization grows.

The initial goal in this relationship will be to secure a "Letter of Approval" from the SSA that gives permission for the RPO to charge a fee for their services. Each year the SSA determines how much can be charged. In 2010, a RPO can charge $37 per month per beneficiary. If the beneficiary receives less than $370 from the SSA each month, the charge can be no more than 10 percent of the income received.

This fee serves two purposes. First, it helps underwrite the cost of the RPO. Second, the beneficiary is paying for a service. This adds to their self-worth and the value of your services to them. Even though the organization has complete control over their income, they have the right to expect dependable service as well as an encouraging relationship.

The First Five Beneficiaries

The first step toward acquiring a Letter of Approval is to sign up five beneficiaries, budget with them, and manage their income so they have adequate shelter, food, and clothing. The actual signing up of the first five clients is the hardest step in all of the processes and the person designated by the Board to actually do this must be focused and tenacious.

Signing up five clients, starting their accounts, and following the SSA procedures is necessary to prove to the SSA that the new organization and the person responsible for managing the organization is capable of being a representative payee. This is one of the most difficult steps toward receiving a Letter of Approval, but having a fee base to support a large part of the RPO's budget makes it worthwhile in many ways.

Beneficiaries of another RPO usually will not be reassigned by the SSA to a new RPO, so the key is to find beneficiaries who need a representative payee and are willing to cooperate. Beneficiaries who are disgruntled with their present representative payee or a representative payee who cannot manage the beneficiaries' income are good possibilities. In some cases a family member becomes a representative payee and then, since money and control are necessary, arguments and anger enter into the relationship. An outsider can relieve this tension in the family by becoming the representative payee.

Contacting the director of a homeless center or Rescue Mission can be a source for finding the first beneficiaries. Around 60 percent of those frequenting these ministries receive SSA support. Not all will respond to having a representative payee, but I have discovered there are a few who want to live a more fulfilling life. It takes time to cultivate their trust and the one or two who respond must find the new RPO trustworthy. Word of mouth endorsement about your caring help will be your best advertisement.

The Board of Directors should help in finding the first five beneficiaries. They can tell friends and work colleagues about the project and the need. Churches should be told about the new ministry and asked to pray for these first clients. It is startling to find out how many people in the congregation are serving as an individual representative payee for a challenged friend or family member. With these contacts, the RPO's representative must develop trust, explain the new development and ask if it would be helpful to them to have a neutral RPO manage the beneficiary's income.

Beneficiaries are always reluctant to change if they think they are going to be charged a fee. They know that an individual representative payee cannot charge a fee, but a RPO can make the charge. It is best to promise the first five beneficiaries they will never be charged a fee for the services of the new RPO if they sign up.

If the new RPO is clearly legally established in the community, submitting a Form 11 and 4164 to the local Social Security office should be adequate. But if the local manager of the Social Security office requires otherwise, the representative of the RPO will have to take the new beneficiaries to the local Social Security office and fill out the forms. Each beneficiary will have to declare to the Social Security representative that he/she definitely wishes to change from their present representative payee to the new RPO.

The Social Security representative should understand this is a new RPO. The RPO representative should use the RPO's name and E.I.N. and sign as the person responsible for the administration of the program.

Letter of Approval

When the RPO has five beneficiaries, the next step is to apply at the SSA for a Letter of Approval. This letter has three benefits for the RPO. First is the right to charge each beneficiary of the RPO's service a fee.

The second benefit is the right to an audit. There are two levels of accounting in the office of a RPO. The first level is the accounting for the incomes received and expenses paid for beneficiaries. The second level is the receipts and expenses of the business side of the organization. The SSA audits the first level. A private audit needs to be arranged for the second level. When all of the accounts are kept in an orderly manner, all audits are helpful and will help sharpen the organization.

The third benefit is respect and a closer working relationship with the personnel of the local Social Security office. Since the RPO is recognized by the local Social Security office, work that would normally require a person going to the Social Security office can be accomplished in the RPO's office. Telephoning, faxing, mailing, and submitting documents on-line are made possible with this letter.

In order to obtain a Letter of Approval and have the right to collect a fee for services, the RPO must request authorization in writing from the local Social Security office. Again, there is a process that needs to be followed.

When the RPO has organized to the point of starting to recruit the first five clients, send a one page letter of intent to the director of the Social Security office that services the zip code address in which the RPO's office is located. In a few sentences tell about the organization and point out that you are in the process of signing up the first five beneficiaries.

In this letter, it is imperative you mention that this RPO is interested in working with those who are challenged. This would include individuals who are homeless, abused, bipolar, schizophrenic, or have a dual diagnosis with self medication and resulting substance addictions. This points out that this RPO will not pick and choose the easiest beneficiaries, but that the goal is to work with the SSA to serve those who are truly marginalized.

In the letter, ask for the SSA requirements for a RPO receiving a Letter of Approval. If the Director replies, you have established a rapport. If the director does not reply, then you will need to recruit a politically important person in the community to help make an appointment after you have your organization in order and have signed up five beneficiaries. It is important to be focused on your purpose and thoughtfully tenacious when responses from the SSA are lethargic.

When the incomes of five beneficiaries are being managed, the 12 items listed below must be hand carried and submitted to the director of the local Social Security office by the principal individuals organizing the RPO. The presence of a well-known public person helps. Even though some of these items are not specifically requested in any of the SSA manuals, individuals studying the request will ask for them.

1. Form SSA-445. This two page form is not on-line and must be obtained from the local Social Security office. It is self-explanatory and must be completely filled out.

2. Articles of Incorporation. On the first page the name of the

corporation and the purpose of the RPO should be lightly high-lighted with a highlighter.

3. By-laws.

4. A copy of the IRS letter assigning the E.I.N. to this RPO.

5. A copy of the letter giving the RPO tax-exempt, 501(c)3, status.

6. A statement of the RPO's general service area. Starting with where the organization's office is located, this area can be a section of the city or a part of the county. Make certain it includes marginalized areas from which the majority of your clients will come. Do not include areas that other Social Security offices service. Go on-line and look up the zip code area served by the Social Security office with whom you are working. When RPOs bring in work from other areas, it is not appreciated and cooperation fades quickly. When a RPO carries part of the work load of the local Social Security office, cooperation takes root and grows. Beneficiaries can be accepted from areas serviced by other Social Security offices, but the correspondence has to be with the appropriate office.

7. List the names, Social Security Numbers, and addresses of the clients you are presently serving.

8. Give a total of the client funds your RPO is managing. This should include a total of the beneficiary incomes, residual funds not being used, savings, and dedicated funds.

9. Include a certificate of liability insurance with a specific summary of the insurance coverage. It should include a bond for crime that includes: employee theft; premises; in transit; forgery; computer fraud; and funds transfer fraud. The bond coverage should be higher than the total of all beneficiary funds being managed. It should also show coverage for a growth potential of 50 clients. This certificate is available upon demand from your insurance company.

10. A copy of the RPO's current license. In California the State Board of Equalization issues what is called an Organizational Clearance Certificate. To apply for this certificate, form BOE-267 can be obtained at the county assessor's office. This form must be

filed by February 15th of each year. The purpose of this certificate is to declare any income from any part of the property the RPO is occupying.

11. A statement assuring SSA that the RPO is not charging the beneficiaries a fee, and will not charge them a fee until there is a Letter of Approval issued, and that when the Letter of Approval is issued the RPO will not make the fees retroactive.

12. A statement designating who will sign all documents and checks for the RPO and the clients. It is good to have the same signature on a stamp and present that stamped signature at the same time.

This material is given to the Director of the local Social Security office. After the Director is satisfied the necessary information has been submitted, it will be sent to the SSA regional office. It will then be forwarded to the SSA in Baltimore, Maryland, for final approval.

When the RPO has a Letter of Approval and the right to charge a fee, Social Security offices can then make referrals to the RPO. The referrals are made when the Director of the local Social Security office determines that a recipient of Social Security benefits is too challenged or incapable, due to physical, emotional, or relational problems, to use their benefits appropriately. The beneficiary's funds will be stopped and they will be requested to find a representative payee. If they need a RPO, a paper giving the name and address of the RPO, will be handed to them as a referral.

As the number of beneficiaries grows, the staff of the RPO will be regularly corresponding, faxing, telephoning, and visiting the Social Security office. The paperwork will be frustrating at times, but frustration should not become a major part of the relationship between the two offices. In spite of differences and mistakes, the desire should be to enhance the work of one another for the best interest of those being served.

Every other year, Social Security personnel will audit the work of the RPO. You will be given a list of names a few days in advance and be asked to have their files ready for the audit. The auditors will go over them very carefully and write up their findings.

Every so often, Social Security personnel should be invited to visit the RPO to meet with the staff and have a time of questions and answers. The basic question is, "How can we better serve one another?"

Banking

Never assume your banker understands your banking needs. They understand the systems and products the bank is offering to the public, but need a thoughtful explanation of your program's banking needs in order to integrate them into the bank's systems.

There are two different banking programs offered by banks to RPOs. First is a single checking account into which all of the beneficiaries direct deposits are made. This is commonly called a global account. Second is the provision of individual fiduciary checking accounts, opened to receive the direct deposit of each beneficiary's income.

The system we have observed that seems to always culminate in disaster is the single account or global account. This program permits the RPO to open one account for all of their clients' direct deposits. This means all clients' deposits and withdrawals are made from the same account.

The banker's point is that from this global deposit, any trained person can determine, with help from the bank, the correct amount that belongs to each client. Accounts for each beneficiary will be set up in the RPO's office and it is there that the record will be kept of how much money belongs to each beneficiary. The checks for the needs of the beneficiaries can be written out of the global account but recorded in the individual beneficiary's account maintained in the RPO's office.

Three negative occurrences seem to plague the global bank account system. First is human error and client fraud. Social Security, bank, and RPO personnel make mistakes. It cannot be avoided.

Besides this, every once in a while a client will change or forge a check. When either of these happens in a global system, it can take weeks to discover the problem. Sometimes the system has to be closed down, an audit taken, and accounts have to be balanced. One agency in our area had to close because minor errors had escalated to the point where there was no way of going back and balancing the account.

The second negative occurrence that can cause this system to fail is fraud. Three hundred clients can mean $300,000 in a global account. When beneficiaries do not use all of their income in the month it was deposited, there is a buildup of residual funds in the account. This money still belongs to individual beneficiaries, but the build-up in the account makes it easy to borrow from Peter to pay Paul. Desperate situations in the lives of beneficiaries or in the life of the RPO can create a huge temptation to borrow money out of the global account. Most pay back agendas do not work and the global account soon has a negative balance that will make it impossible to fully serve the beneficiaries. Eventually this negative balance will show up in an audit.

The third negative occurrence, that can frustrate the beneficiaries, is the time needed for recording on the separate beneficiary accounts, in the RPO's office, the amount deposited in the global account at the bank. It takes a lot of time to take apart a global account and see how much was actually deposited for each beneficiary. This means that rents and bills can get paid late and beneficiaries, needing food and other necessities, become angry and frustrated when they have to wait for their personal checks.

The SSA makes the deposits available at midnight on the day the beneficiaries are to receive their income. With individual accounts at the bank, the RPO representative, having access to these accounts, can immediately tell how much was deposited and serve the beneficiaries.

SSA requires each client to have a separate account. It is incredible that this requirement is often passed over because of pressure from the banks to use a global account.

Having individual accounts is a policy of Stewards Inc. As a result of this policy, on the first of the month, when almost $1,500,000 is deposited in 1,600 accounts, the employees of Stewards Inc are able to open the doors at 8:00 AM and generate checks in confidence that each account will balance to the penny._

Individual accounts for each beneficiary are generally not profitable for a bank since the funds deposited are in and out in the span of a month. They can be slightly profitable, however, if the employees of a RPO avoid errors in their banking. Monthly deposits have to be verified on-line before checks are written. Checks should be written according to the budget agreed upon by each beneficiary. For those accounts that are drawn down each month, $3 to $5 should always remain in the account and carry over to the next month. No reason should be accepted for writing a check that would leave a negative balance. If a beneficiary loses a check or it is stolen and a request is made for a stop payment, the beneficiary must pay the stop payment fee. If an employee of the RPO makes a mistake and there is a bank charge, the RPO should pay the charge. If some of the beneficiary's income is lost due to a mistake, the RPO should reimburse the lost funds. Careful, error free work, saves losses for the bank, the beneficiary, and the RPO.

Office Procedures

The physical arrangement of the office, procedures for relating to clients, and systems used to process incomes and paperwork should all be organized from the client's point of view. It is like any other business. When the customers are happy, everything runs much more smoothly. Some beneficiaries feel good about the help they receive, while others chaff under the idea that someone else is controlling their income. There are always those who are difficult because of their mental challenges and addictions and can be disruptive and abusive. Organizing a user friendly RPO will eliminate a lot of frustration and help the purpose of the RPO to be realized.

The physical arrangement of the Stewards Inc office is intentional and unique. The office is totally open with only the restrooms, break room, small conference room, and storeroom having walls. 25 percent of the room has chairs for clients and 75 percent of the room has desks neatly organized for the employees. Each desk has a chair for the client to be seated while being served. All employees work in this open space. Dividing the waiting area and work area is a low long desk where one can be seated on either side to converse. Everyone in the room is visible. Those coming to the office can pick up a check at the counter, sign in to see a specific person, or sign in and see whichever client representative is available.

There are three reasons for the open office policy. First, beneficiaries do not wonder what the client representatives are doing while they are waiting. Second, the employees can observe any problems with the beneficiaries such as drug or alcohol use. Third, there is no corner where a beneficiary can quickly corner a client representative or take something from a desk.

Most offices assign a certain number of beneficiaries to each employee. At Stewards Inc we only assign the few who are disruptive or tend to emotionally melt down to a specific client representative. This is about 10 percent of the beneficiaries. If that client representative is not present, the beneficiary is not turned away.

The other 90 percent of the beneficiaries see the next client representative who is available.

This means that every change, problem or question must be noted in the beneficiaries' hardback folder or in the computer.

In an office with only thirty beneficiaries, the one client representative can do everything. As time goes by, and staff and business grows, administrative functions must be assigned to different client representatives. The following list is not an exhaustive list of administrative tasks, but it covers the basics for a well-run office:

1. Receiving the beneficiaries' incomes and paying their bills is a major part of the business' product or service. Both of these processes involve keeping a very clear picture of the flow of money

through bookkeeping.

2. Preparing deposits, opening and closing accounts, and processing problems related to banking require an understanding of the very stringent rules that govern banking. The bank usually assigns one person to process the RPO'S accounts and it is best to have one person in the RPO's office taking care of the banking.

3. Signing up new beneficiaries involves listening to their story, organizing their needs into a budget, acquainting them with the organization's policies, and helping them understand the timeline for papers being processed and their income becoming available. Besides the forms required by the SSA to complete this process, there is a contract to be signed by the new client and the RPO representative as to what each one can expect in the way of treatment.

There are two problems that immediately surface and the person signing up the beneficiary must have a clear solution. First is the question, "When do I get my money?" It must be explained that if Social Security receives their papers before the 18th or 19th of the month, there is a good chance that their new RPO will become their representative payee and will receive their check on the first of the next month. If their check does not arrive on the first of the month and there was a former representative payee, the check probably went to the former representative payee. If there was no former representative payee, then the RPO will have to petition the local Social Security office for an emergency check.

The second problem is the beneficiary becoming attached to the person signing them up. This is the first person in the office they meet. If it was a cordial, productive meeting, they will feel this is the only person who can help them. It needs to be clearly explained that any person in the office can help them.

4. Maintaining a strong relationship with SSA is vital in order to process the myriad of problems that arise. Respond to all SSA letters received, and prepare the reports requested. Overall, during a year, millions of dollars are involved and the paperwork the SSA requests is their attempt to make sure funds are used wisely and there is ad-

equate accounting. Out of respect for the staff at Social Security, it is best to have one person at the RPO making the telephone calls and keeping track of the requests and forms that require action.

5. About four percent of the RPO's beneficiaries are incarcerated at any one time. These beneficiaries remain a client for a year and the RPO is responsible to freeze their income and submit the proper forms to the SSA. A fee cannot be collected during this time.

Other beneficiaries are on probation, have a warrant out for their arrest, or have fines that must be paid. It takes one staff person who understands the regulations of the courts as well as the guidelines of SSA to keep these monies and records in order.

6. There is a series of reports required by SSA that relate to the well-being of those on disability. To fill them out requires interviewing the beneficiary and going over their records. If these are not completed in a timely manner, their income stops. One staff member is needed to schedule the processing of these reports since many beneficiaries forget appointments or neglect to furnish needed information.

7. Seniors who are required to sign up with a RPO often have no one in their lives who will help them as they age. Maintaining Medicare and medical benefits is a daunting task. Social Security and other agencies will give training on understanding and using these programs.

One client representative needs to specialize in helping these clients through the stages of care that are required for their well-being. When they can no longer live alone, they need to be helped as they move from their house or apartment to room and board, board and care, nursing facility, and finally a hospital. There are forms for each one of these stages. When they die there are appropriate reports to be filled out and personal belongings to be dealt with. This responsibility takes compassion, an understanding of the related laws, and familiarity with the required forms to be processed.

8. It is best to have all of the beneficiaries' bills mailed directly to the RPO's office. The few who keep their bills will often manipu-

late or negate their budget. In the office, a hardback folder for each client needs to be maintained in order that bills can be filed properly and made ready for payment. After the bills are paid, another set of files needs to be maintained on a yearly basis as a paper trail for the checks written. Deadlines for the payment of all bills must be honored so as not to incur penalties.

9. Most beneficiaries get the remainder of their income, after rents and bills are paid, in weekly checks. If they cannot manage weekly checks, they will receive two checks a week or even one a day. Often checks are made out to grocery stores or other merchants and the purpose of the check is written in the check memo to discourage its misuse. Social Security requests the RPO place in savings a small percent of the beneficiaries' income each month. This would be for special needs. This savings is not mandatory, but about 20 percent of the beneficiaries are able to save a little.

10. Maintaining orderly files expedites the monthly processes for serving beneficiaries and keeps a traceable paper trail for all monies received and all checks written. A hardback file for each beneficiary holds all of the records that are used monthly. Bills to be paid are filed in this file. Soft files are maintained for each client as a place to keep all bills after they are paid and bank statements after the accounts are balanced. At the end of each year, the soft files are boxed up and a new set of soft files are instituted. The soft files can be shredded after seven years.

11. All accounting is kept on computers.

Major Forms and Contracts Used by a RPO

The following list of forms is not exhaustive, but these forms are the backbone of working with Social Security. Many other forms can be filled out on-line and sent back to the SSA. Examples would be a notification of death, replacement for a lost Medicare or medical card, or a request for direct deposit.

Signing up a new Beneficiary:

SSA 4164   must be signed by the beneficiary and submitted with form SSA 11. The beneficiary is declaring that they accept this organization as their RPO.

SSA 11   is a request from the RPO to the SSA that this organization be selected as the representative payee for the beneficiary who signed the accompanying form SSA 4164. Only the first four pages of SSA 11 are turned into the local SSA office.

Other SSA forms frequently used:

SSA 16   should be filled out by a person seeking disability support from the SSI program. It is best for that person to go into the local Social Security office and request this form. The date of the request is recorded by SSA in their records. If the disability of this person is accepted after a 9 to 12 month period of time, back pay to the date the forms were issued will be paid.

SSA 632   is a request for a waiver or forgiveness of an overpayment. Sometimes SSA will overpay a beneficiary and want the overpayment returned. If there is a good reason it cannot be repaid over time, this form is used to declare that it would be a hardship. If SSA agrees, the overpayment is forgiven.

SSA 8202 & 8203	are statement forms for determining the continued eligibility of a beneficiary for SSI payments. Periodically these are sent out to the RPO to be filled out. Those who need the SSI support the most seem to be the beneficiaries who are the hardest to bring to the office to fill out the forms. Failure to return the forms in due time can cost the beneficiary their benefits.
SSA 789	is submitted if a beneficiary feels they have lost their benefits unfairly.
SSA 454	is submitted if the review culminates in a decision to deny benefits.

Contracts:

There are two contracts that need to be signed by the new beneficiary and a representative of the RPO. They are found on-line and in the SSA handbook for RPOs. Collectively they declare the new beneficiary has had the process of managing their income explained to them, the way they should conduct themselves in the office, and the treatment they will receive from office personnel.

May this guide be a useful tool in the development of your ministry.

BIBLIOGRAPHY

Affordable Housing Shrinks, HUD. "Waiting Lists Grow While Affordable Housing Shrinks." http://www.huduser.org/periodicals/rrr/rrr5_99art1.html [accessed July 12, 2007].

Bakke, Ray. *A Theology as Big as the City.* Downers Grove: Inter Varsity Press, 1997.

Barak, Gregg. *Gimme Shelter, A Social History of Homelessness in Contemporary America.* New York: Praeger Brothers, 1992.

Barclay, William. *The Gospel of Matthew, Volume 1.* Revised Edition. Philadelphia: The Westminster Press, 1975.

Bright, John. *The Kingdom of God.* Nashville: Abingdon, 1953.

A History of Israel, Third Edition. Philadelphia: Westminster Press, 1981.

Catholic Charities, USA-Providing Help. Creating Hope. "History of Catholic Charities USA." www.catholiccharitiesusa.org [accessed October 29, 2008].

"Charitable Choice: The Facts, The White House, Faith-Based and Community Initiatives." http://www.whitehouse.gov/government/fbci/guidance.charitable.html [accessed September 22, 2008].

"Compassion Fatigue Awareness Project." http://www.compassion-fatigue.org [accessed September 3, 2008].

Conrad, Kendon J., Michael D. Matters, Patricia Hanrahan, Daniel J. Luchins, Courtenay Savage, and Betty Daugherty. "Characteristics of Persons with Mental Illness in a Representative Payee Program."

Dahm, Charles W. *Parish Ministry in a Hispanic Community.* New York/Mahwah: Paulist Press, 2004.

Dinsmore, Paul C. and Jeannette Casbanis-Brown. *The AMA Handbook of Project Management.* New York:Amacombooks, 2006.

Dybek, Styart. *The Coast of Chicago (a collection of short stories about neighborhood life in Chicago's southwest side).* U.S.A.: Picador, 2003.

Earley, Pete. *Crazy A Father's Search Through America's Mental Health Madness.* New York: Berkley Books, 2006.

Elbogen, Eric B., Joelle C. Ferron, Marvin S. Swartz, Christine M. Wilder, Jeffrey W. Swanson, and H. Ryan Wagner. "Characteristics of Representative Payeeship involving Families with Psychiatric Disabilities." *Psychiatric Services,* (Nov. 1, 2007) 58 (11): 1433-1440.

Equal Treatment for Faith-Based Providers. "Faith-Based and Community Initiatives: Guidance – Equal Treatment." http://www.whitehouse.gov/government/fbci/guidance/equal.html [accessed September 15, 2008].

Feldman, Noah. *Divided By God.* New York: Farrar, Straus, and Giroux, 2005.

Fuder, John. *A Heart for the City: Effective Ministries to the Urban*

Community. Chicago: Moody Press, 1999.

Gordon, Wayne L. *Real Hope in Chicago.* Grand Rapids: Zondervan Publishing House, 1997.

"Government Partners: Navigating Charitable Choice." http://www.religion-online.org/showarticle.asp?title=2027 [accessed September 18, 2008].

Green Clifford J. *Churches, Cities, and Human Community: Urban Ministry in the United States 1945-1985.* Grand Rapids: William B. Eerdmans, 1998.

Guder, Darrell L. *Missional Church, A Vision for the Sending of the Church in North America.* Grand Rapids: William B. Eerdmans, 1998.

"History of the Association of Gospel Rescue Missions." http://www.agrm.org/history.html [accessed January 19, 2009].

"History of Lutheran Social Services." http://www.lsswis.org/AboutUs/history.html [accessed October 30, 2008].

HHS CFBCI. "The President's Initiative and HHS." http://www.hhs.gov/fbci/president.html [accessed February 16, 2009].

Homelessness in the United States. "Historical Background." http://en.wikipedia.org/wiki/Homelessness [accessed February 8, 2006].

Kennedy, Sheila Suess. *Privatization and Prayer: The challenge of Charitable Source.* A manuscript filed at the University of Indiana, undated.

Ladd, George Eldon. *A Theology of the New Testament.* Grand Rapids: William B. Eerdmans, 1974.

Lamb, Richard H. and Linda E. Weinberger. "The Shift of Psychiatric Inpatient Care From Hospitals to Jails and Prisons." *Journal of the American Academy of Psychiatry Law,* (2005) 33:4: 529-534.

Linthicum, Robert. *Transforming Power, Biblical Strategies for Making a Difference in Your Community.* Downer's Grove: Inter Varsity Press, 2003.

Luchins, Daniel J., Patricia Hanrahan, Kendon J. Conrad, Courtenay Savage, Michael D. Matters, Marc Shinderman. "An Agency-Based Representative Payee Program And Improved Community Tenure of Persons With Mental Illness." *Psychiatric Services* (September, 1998): 1218-1222.

Lupton, Robert D. *Compassion, Justice and the Christian Life, re-thinking Ministry to The Poor.* Ventura: Regal, 2007.

National Research Council, *Improving the Social Security Representative Payee Program, Serving Beneficiaries and Minimizing Misuse.* Washington, D.C.: The National Academies Press, 2007.

"Partnering with Faith-based and Community Organizations." http://www.whitehouse.gov./government/fbci/guidance/partnering.html [accessed February 15, 2009].

Poor House Story Home Page. "History, Poor Houses by State." http://www.poorhousestory.com [accessed January 6, 2007].

"Proselytism." http://www.answers.com/proselytism [accessed March 13, 2009].

Rollisom, Paul A. and John T. Pardock. *Homelessness in rural America, Policy and Practice.* New York: The Haworth Press, Inc., 2006.

"The Salvation Army." http://en.wikipedia.org/wiki/Salvation_ Army#United_States [accessed October 30, 2008].

Separation of Church and State. "History of the Concept and Term." http://en.wikipedia.org/wiki.Separation_of_church_and _state [accessed September 14, 2008].

Separation of Church and State. " Modern Views." http:// en.wikipedia.org/wiki.Separation_of_church_and_State [accessed September 10, 2008].

Shavelson, Lonny. *Hooked, Five Addicts Challenge Our Misguided Drug Rehab System.* New York: the New Press, 2001.

Smith, Brad, "Transformational Leadership." Lecture at Bakke Graduate University, Seattle, WA, June 8, 2004.

Social Security Administration, A Guide For Representative Payees, SSA Publication No. 05-10076.

Social Security Administration, Office of Beneficiary and Determination Services, *Representative Payee Program, Guide for Organizational Representative Payees, 2008,* SSA Pulication No. 17-013.

Social Security Administration. Research, Statistics, and Policy Analysis. "Quick Facts, Monthly Statistical Snapshot." http://

www.ssa.gov/policy/ [accessed December 8, 2008].

Social Security Online History Pages. "Historical Background and Development of Social Security." http://www.social security. gov/history [accessed October 28, 2008].

U.S. Census Bureau-Poverty. "Detailed Poverty Tables." http:// www.census.gov/hhes/www/poverty.html [accessed January 8, 2008].

Swindoll, Charles R. and Roy B. Zuck. *Understanding Christian Theology.* Nashville: Thomas Nelson, 2003.

Venkatesh, Sudhir Alladi. *Off the Books. The Underground Economy of the Urban Poor.* Cambridge: Harvard University Press, 2006.

Von Hoffman, Alexander *House by House, Block by Block, the Rebirth of America's Urban Neighborhood.* New York: Oxford University Press, 2003.

Wellman Jr., James K. *The Gold Coast Church and the Ghetto: Christ and Culture in Mainline Protestantism.* Urbana and Chicago: University of Illinois Press, 1999.

Breinigsville, PA USA
28 August 2010
244405BV00002B/1/P